STATE OF NEW YORK

REPORT

OF AN

Investigation of the Municipal Civil Service Commission and of the Administration of the Civil Service Law and Rules

IN THE

CITY OF NEW YORK

TRANSMITTED TO THE LEGISLATURE FEBRUARY 1, 1915

ALBANY
J. B. LYON COMPANY, PRINTERS
1915

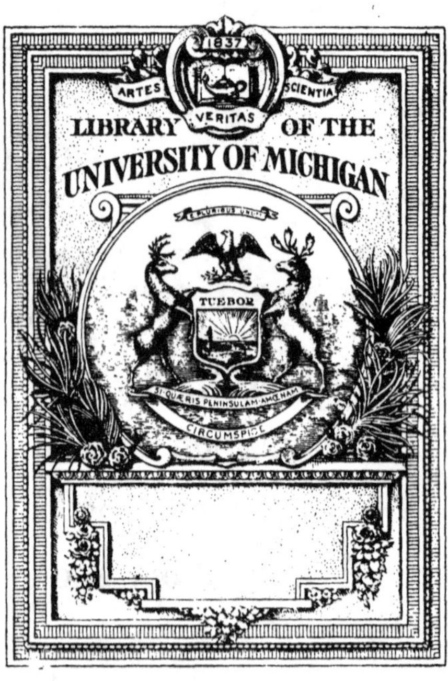
1837
ARTES
VERITAS
SCIENTIA
LIBRARY OF THE
UNIVERSITY OF MICHIGAN
TUEBOR
SI QUÆRIS PENINSULAM AMŒNAM
CIRCUMSPICE

STATE OF NEW YORK

REPORT

OF AN

Investigation of the Municipal Civil Service Commission and of the Administration of the Civil Service Law and Rules

IN THE

CITY OF NEW YORK

TRANSMITTED TO THE LEGISLATURE FEBRUARY 1, 1915

ALBANY
J. B. LYON COMPANY, PRINTERS
1915

STATE OF NEW YORK

No. 35

IN SENATE

FEBRUARY 1, 1915

Report of an Investigation of the Municipal Civil Service Commission and of the Administration of the Civil Service Law and Rules in the City of New York

STATE OF NEW YORK

OFFICE OF STATE CIVIL SERVICE COMMISSION

ALBANY, N. Y., *January* 28, 1915

Though an examination of each local civil service commission is required to be made at least once in two years, it appears that no formal inspection of any matter has been made in New York city for nine years, and that no general examination has been made within present memory.

As this Commission began to consider the duty of examining civil service conditions in municipalities, its attention was directed to the many exceptions and exemptions from examination made by the New York City Civil Service Commission, and the numerous requests of the local officials for rulings which required the concurrence of the State Civil Service Commission. Such concurrence had been freely given, relying upon the judgment and care of the local commission, until abuse became apparent and curtailment necessary. This abuse reached a climax when the municipal commission permitted the appointment of forty-seven examiners of charitable institutions ignoring an appropriate eligible list containing 110 names.

The spirit and letter of article V, section 9 of the Constitution was evaded and ignored by this action. This section is as follows:

> " Appointments and promotions in the civil service of the state, and of all the civil divisions thereof, including cities and villages, shall be made according to merit and fitness to be ascertained, so far as practicable, by examinations, which, so far as practicable, shall be competitive; provided, however, that honorably discharged soldiers and sailors from the army and navy of the United States in the late civil war, who are citizens and residents of this state, shall be entitled to preference in appointment and promotion, without regard to their standing on any list from which such appointment or promotion may be made. Laws shall be made to provide for the enforcement of this section."

On the appearance of the State Commission in the City of New York, to undertake its examination of the records, it began to receive complaints in large numbers from individuals and from societies, specifying violations and evasions of the Civil Service Law in many departments, and the duty of this Commission to make an investigation soon became evident. The State Commission learning that the city officials would have the assistance of the corporation counsel, requested the Attorney-General to assign counsel to its service. He did secure and designate Frank Moss of New York city as a special deputy and Mr. Moss has remained with this Commission throughout the inquiry; the city officials being represented at times by the corporation counsel, Frank L. Polk, and constantly by his assistant Josiah Stover and by special counsel Frederic R. Coudert, and near the end also by Howard Gans.

Early in the inquiry one of the prominent commissioners of the city, who claimed to be advised by the corporation counsel, challenged the right of this Commission to require the attendance of employees of his department by subpoena except at regular sessions of the Commission, and recognizing the antagonism of some of the officials towards the proposed inquiry, it was determined to make the proceedings absolutely formal and to give privileges not usually accorded in investigations. All the testimony reported herewith was taken in open public session, and was reported by competent stenographers and full transcripts thereof were furnished from day to day to the local commission at the expense of the State Commission. The fullest privilege of counsel was accorded; cross-examination at length was permitted; at many points in the inquiry officials were permitted to take the stand and to present witnesses to explain matters. The engagements of counsel in court and elsewhere were recognized and adjournments were frequently granted. Counsel for the city officials many times stated their desire to have two days at the end for rebuttal not perfected as the inquiry progressed, and six days were allowed by this Commission, with the expressed willingness to hold night sessions for the uses of the said officials.

At the end of the inquiry on January 22d, the corporation counsel requested another week for further rebuttal, which request we were compelled to deny, because our resignations to take effect on February 1, 1915, had been forwarded to the Governor and it was clear to us that the intervening week would be needed to formulate and present our report.

At a meeting of the State Commission held September 18, 1914, the formal investigation was ordered under the authority vested by section 6, subdivision 3 of the Civil Service Law. Between September 29, 1914, and January 22, 1915, we held forty-five sessions, and an inspection of the record will show how fully the privilege of cross-examining and of rebutting was accorded, and how large a proportion of the time was taken by the cross-examinations, the testimony, the speeches and the exhibits offered by the local department heads.

It has been the earnest desire of this Commission to conduct an inquiry which would be fair to the local officials, free from prejudice and partisanship, and likely to benefit the city, the State and the army of public servants. There has been no design to discredit the local administration as some have declared; but we have desired rather to aid it to become a shining exponent of true civil service policies and practices. While there have been points where opinions clashed, yet there have been many instances where the local commissioners were in accord with us, and expressed appreciation of our help in revealing conditions which had not been recognized or realized by them and it is fair to say that this Commission has found no evidence of malfeasance in the local board, and that some of the matters criticized have come down from earlier administrations unchecked by any action of former State Civil Service Commissions, which evidently have refrained from investigating the New York City Commission through fear of attack for interference. The nonpartisanship of our inquiry was safeguarded by the bipartisan character of our organization, for two of the commissioners are Democrats, while the other commissioner and the counsel are Republicans; all have been in unanimous and hearty agreement throughout the proceeding.

While the inquiry has centered about the municipal commission, it has included a large part of the public service, and has comprised the whole field of civil service. So wide an inquiry has not been accomplished easily and has provoked resentment in some quarters.

Violations of the law and of the spirit of the law have been found in many offices and departments, some, to the expressed surprise of the local commission. In several notable instances specified hereafter, the local commission has amended and improved its methods in particulars revealed by the hearing.

Some of the violations of law are of long standing and have continued without apparent effort to discover or to correct them. This is not strange, for the local commission itself has violated the law in many particulars. These violations have produced a distrust of the merit system in many persons, and a belief that the law is manipulated for favorites or to accomplish certain ends. At our very last session Commissioner Keogh voluntarily stated in substance that the local commission realize that they have been imposed upon by heads of departments in their applications for exception of particular appointees, and that special plans have been formulated lately by which the Commission will proceed to inform itself of the qualifications of candidates for exception and not be compelled to rely upon the statements of commissioners who desire to make the appointments.

The general administration of the city and the character of its officials are so high, that an example of laxity or of unfair uses of the powers and resources of the law, is unfortunate. Under such an administration civil employees and those who aspire to public employment should have no doubt that the law will be obeyed in its spirit and purpose. The exponents of unselfish good government should set an example in administering the Civil Service Law in the interest of all the people and all the employees rather than for the benefit of heads of departments and personal friends.

Exemptions and Exceptions

We endeavored to ascertain the number of employees who had been excepted from examination during 1914 under Rule 12. The local commission up to the last session stated its inability to make a complete answer to our inquiry. It furnished the names of 621 persons, and said there were many more whom they could not tabulate for want of time. Commissioner Keogh at the last session made a long statement of the reasons for many of the exceptions under paragraph 6, and it was evident that the desires of the heads of departments who wished the exception of candidates had generally prevailed without independent inquiry by the civil service commission. Some of these exceptions will be discussed under appropriate heads.

Unfair and Faulty Examinations of Candidates

Many complaints of unfair examinations were made to this commission. We were compelled to give considerable time to the subject, though we closed with much unused material.

1. *Physical.* In the report of the municipal commission to the mayor dated July 1, 1914, it was said "A more rigid standard of physical requirements has been adopted upon the ground that the municipal departments should be manned by the physically fit and that the employment of the unfit is not the direction in which the city should express its charity." * * *

> "A complete set of standards of physical requirements are being formulated, showing in detail the physical conditions required for all positions subject to examination. It is the

intention of this Commission to publish these standards of physical requirements in such form that any candidate may know before examination what physical qualifications are necessary."

The good intentions of the commissioners have been executed in such ill-balanced and impractical ways as to produce confusion and to work injustice to many persons.

a. Tests for policemen and firemen remain practically as they were.

b. When large numbers of applicants have appeared, as in the finger-print expert examination, requirements have been increased — for instance, alleged flat-foot was an insuperable barrier, though the applicant was successfully operating as finger-print examiner in a magistrate's court under temporary appointment.

c. In certain examinations the printed announcements have stated requirements such as freedom of heart and lungs from organic disease, freedom from flat-foot, varicose veins, hernia, etc., and yet no proper or sufficient tests have been applied to the candidates to determine these conditions. No doubt many were deterred by the printed announcements which were ignored.

d. The lifting of a 40-pound dumb-bell has been required of candidates for mental alienists and finger-print experts, with examinations of feet, legs, heart and lungs; while for other positions 30-pound dumb-bells have sufficed, and for such a position as foreman of sewer cleaners, whose occupation is trying and hazardous, no examination whatever for heart, lungs, legs and feet has been given.

e. There are two physical tests which bar the way to all positions: these are (1) the test of picking up and raising a 30 or 40-pound dumb-bell above the head; (2) the ability to read a line or more from a chart of No. "20" letters, at a distance of 20 feet. The candidate may do this with or without glasses, and as to glasses, he may use magnifiers or window glass, it makes no difference. In the great majority of the examinations, these are the only tests, except such cursory observation as the attending physician may make of the candidates as they approach and pass him on line — large numbers in a room, and men or women passing rapidly, so that each candidate has passed his two tests in about five minutes.

We found numerous cases, where candidates in obvious good health and efficiency were blocked by the inability to elevate the dumb-bell above the shoulder (often through lack of the knack of doing it), or through failure to read one or two letters in a line, regardless of the application of those particular tests to the work to be done in the employment.

f. In many cases it was demonstrated to us that the examinations, such as they were, were faulty, and that the rulings of the doctors were erroneous.

g. It was perfectly clear that even among candidates who passed before the doctor's eyes and lifted the dumb-bell, and read the line of letters with or without glasses, that there must have been persons with hernia, and with heart and lung diseases, diseases of the circulation, and many other undisclosed affections.

h. Candidates testified that physical tests were given by persons not physicians, and without the oversight of physicians.

i. The arbitrary requirements of the dumb-bell and the reading chart automatically shut out persons who were efficient, in good health, and of such mental qualities as to make ideal workers.

We found that many rejected candidates appealed to the local commission, and generally their appeals were denied. In the late fall we began to examine the records of physical examinations and to take off the names of rejected candidates, and as some of these were called we discovered that *without appeal, the municipal civil service commission was sending for them, re-examining them, and in many cases, passing them.* On inquiry into the matter we found that the municipal commission became satisfied that the methods in use were working injustice to individuals and stated they were striving to make an improvement. The president expressed his appreciation of the inquiry in this particular and assured us that improvement would be made in this feature of examination.

We have learned that the dumb-bell and eye (chart) tests are as old as 1902, and it is evident that the promise of the report of July 1, 1914, for improved physical examinations has not been fulfilled.

Annexed hereto is *TABLE A*, showing some of the cases under this heading.

Physical Examinations: Policemen and Firemen

Very properly the physical examinations of policemen and firemen are more exacting than those of other civil employees, but they are not different from those of past years. There are physical barriers at the very entrance to the examinations.

The evidence of many candidates shows that the tests of height, weight and strength are given mainly by a clerk named Joseph Ruddy, without the effective oversight of a physician. It is said that he has had experience in athletics, but that does not meet the requirement that a doctor shall give these examinations. A doctor signs the certificates, but on the evidence before us he does not give these tests, and that fact has led to many doubts and criticisms by persons interested in these examinations.

It was impracticable to go very deeply into this subject, but we were able to examine into it sufficiently to ascertain reasons for the distrust that has come to our knowledge.

In heights and weights there are certain arbitrary requirements which seem to be entirely proper; out of which we instance the minimum height of 5 feet 7½ inches, and the minimum weight for that height of 140 pounds. On the examinations given by Mr. Ruddy, we found many candidates who had passed at exactly 5 feet 7½ inches and 140 pounds, we found many failed to pass on the certification by Mr. Ruddy, their height being only 5 feet 7 2/5 inches (a shortage of $\frac{1}{10}$ of an inch); we found some who passed Mr. Ruddy at 5 feet 7 3/5 inches; we found some who failed on 139½ pounds (a shortage of half a pound).

In many cases we found that candidates had called again, and had made up height or weight or both. In some cases disproportion was made up on re-examination by increasing height and reducing weight at the same time, so as to reach the required standard proportion.

In one case a candidate in December, 1913, was measured at 6 feet 3½ inches, and his weight was light for his height; on a remeasurement by Mr. Ruddy in March, 1914, his weight ran up, and his height came down to 6 feet 2½ inches, and he then passed.

On a measurement by Mr. Ruddy for this Commission in November, 1914, the candidate was measured down to 6 feet 1½ inches. This was an apparent shrinkage of the candidate on the standard measuring rod, measured by an expert athlete measurer, of 2 inches within a year, although the candidate said he had tried to stand right each time.

Dr. Warbasse, the chief medical examiner, said this was all right (3217, etc.), quite natural, as were many similar cases with smaller variations. He said it was due to the way the man stood. He and Ruddy both declared that they let the men stand as they will; they give no instruction; the man may present the top back of his head or the top front of his head to the top check of the rod; he may slouch or stiffen up as he pleases, so long as he keeps his feet down; he may have a bump on his head — the measuring rod takes in the bump; he may have thick hair, thin hair or no hair, or may dress up his hair; he may even have his head paddled with a wooden spoon, it is all right.

Mr. Ruddy said that in athletics he had seen candidates carried through the measuring tests by hitting their heads with a spoon. He volunteered the information that he could raise counsel's height by hitting him on the head (scientifically of course). He said, though he had done it in athletics, he never had done it in policemen's or firemen's examinations, but he didn't look too closely at what the men did by way of preparation. (3051-3064, etc.) He said he had reported men to Dr. Warbasse with lumps on their heads and Dr. Warbasse told him to measure them as he found them. (3061.) With this delightful carelessness of preliminary activity, and willingness to take artificial conditions of smart candidates, there goes the arbitrary limitation of the measuring rod so that a shortage of $\frac{1}{10}$ of an inch there, absolutely bars the candidate, no matter what may be his strength, ability and endurance, no matter what his mental and moral qualities.

In many cases new examinations are given in a few months; heights and weights change, eyes are repaired, even flat feet are corrected.

Assistant Chief Examiner Murray testified (p. 3353, etc.), that on November 26, 1913, on his recommendation he was directed by the former municipal civil service commission to make an examination into the methods of holding physical examinations and report possible improvements. He said he visited examinations of patrolmen, and there developed a difference of opinion between him and Dr. Warbasse, and the president (meaning Dr. Moscowitz, see 3357) directed him to discontinue his investigation. He expressed the opinion that a physician should be present at all parts of the physical examination — it did not seem to him this was done. He said, " the biggest part of the physical examining was done by a clerk, Mr. Ruddy." (3356.)

It appeared that the witness had a disagreement with Dr. Warbasse about the general physical examinations (outside of police), and recommended that the advice of the Academy of Medicine be taken. (3359.)

The inquiries by this Commission into specific cases necessarily were limited and hurried, but some very interesting facts will be found in Table B.

Without doubt the methods of examination as formerly conducted by the examiners, still continued, are *faulty,* and the improvements recommended by the Assistant Chief Examiner have *not* been adopted. The re-examinations made under the present Commission in March, 1914, were just as faulty as were the examinations made in 1913, and previously.

Examination for Finger Print Expert

The faults of this examination were found on both the physical and mental sides. The examination was held to supply an eligible list from which to make appointments to half a dozen positions in magistrates' courts which were occupied temporarily. Immediately after its close a large number of the candidates protested to the municipal civil service commission claiming that the examination was faulty and unfair. The local commissioners held an investigation, took testimony, overruled the protests and prepared to promulgate the list and certify persons from it. We stumbled upon this examination through a complaint brought to us by one of the candidates who claimed that he was rejected at the outset for flat-foot, though his feet were all right, and that his appeal to President Moscowitz had been overruled. We found on file a protest specifying a number of irregularities in the examination and signed by forty-nine persons who had entered the examination. On July 27, 1914, President Moscowitz directed a letter to George T. Chattaway, the first objector, as follows:

> "After a thorough investigation of the charges in the petition submitted by your committee relating to the examination for finger print expert, the Commission has come to the conclusion that the charges are without weight."

The State Commission took the testimony of the physicians and examiners who conducted the examination and of a number of persons who were examined and it received written communications from many of the candidates whom it had not time to hear on the stand. On the physical side of the examination surprising inaccuracies and errors were discovered. As already shown, the examination was much more rigorous in physical requirements than were other examinations. Out of the two hundred and ninety-five candidates who appeared for examination, *one hundred and fifty-eight were rejected for alleged physical defects.* Forty-three of these were given re-examinations and of those thirty-eight were again rejected. The examination of individuals by this Commission showed that in many cases the rejections were improper. A considerable part of the physical examination was assisted in by a clerk of the local commission, named Scott, and a police attendant. In a majority of the cases examined by us it appeared that the physical marks were recorded by Mr. Scott on the papers of the candidates, and yet Mr. Scott and the policeman were themselves candidates in the examination, went through all the tests and were examined physically in the presence of some of the very men whom they had examined physically. It appeared that examinations of the feet, legs and chests of men who were candidates, were performed by a woman physician.

The eye-sight tests were peculiar in that some individuals were rejected for defective vision and not told they might use glasses, while others were passed with the aid of glasses. An important element in the eye-sight test was the counting of ridges in the impression of fingers. This was so faulty a test of eye-sight that one of the commissioners, during the investigation, remarked that it was more of a practical test than an eye-sight test. Candidates who were examined by us declared this to be the fact and that candidates had been rejected for alleged imperfect eye-sight when the difficulty was technical as to the starting points and the number of lines to be included. The testimony of one of the examiners, Mr. Taylor (page 6842), made it clear that ridge counting is a technical matter in the classification of finger prints, and that it has to be done under certain regulations which are distinctly expressed at considerable length in the standard text book of Mr. Henry. It was apparent to us that candidates with good eye-sight were turned down upon this test, which, had it been given in the practical examination, would not have counted as an absolute bar but merely as one of the elements in the general marking. Table "C" will show interesting cases under this subject.

On the list which resulted from this examination the first person was a Miss Sullender, the second was Lieutenant Kuhne, who for six years has been a member of Captain Faurot's finger print bureau at police headquarters, and who has been a recognized expert in that bureau, testifying in capital cases. The finger print experts who conducted the examination were Mr. Taylor of the Naval Finger Print Bureau at Washington, D. C., and Dr. De Forrest, one of the regular medical examiners of the Municipal Commission, who has some knowledge of the finger print science. It appeared that Miss Sullender, who was a witness, *had been a nurse in the employ of Dr. DeForrest* and she was employed again on one of his cases after the examination. Some time before the examination occurred, Miss Sullender, with Dr. DeForrest's knowledge, went to Washington and obtained the permission of Mr. Taylor to study in the files of the bureau there. She was assisted by the persons employed in that bureau and for one or two months was present at the bureau about every other day studying and classifying finger prints. She had no previous or other experience in the actual work but had done considerable reading and studying of literature of the subject. At the examination she was recognized by the examiners. In the examination room Miss Sullender had a position which protected her against the delays in the giving out of papers, which handicapped many of the applicants. Her experience paper showed substantially what has been stated and on it she was given a rating of 90 per cent. The experience paper of Lieutenant Kuhne, above referred to, was marked 90 per cent.

In explanation of Miss Sullender's high rating for experience it was stated by Dr. DeForrest that her experience in high school and in a nurses' school entitled her to a higher preliminary rating than could be given to Lieutenant Kuhne, who had only an education obtained in the public schools, in his father's real estate office and as a New York policeman. On examining the papers it was found that another lady, Mrs. Merchant, had superior schooling and had been doing actual finger print work in one of the magistrate's courts; also that she had a wide and varied experience as a stenographer. It was conceded that her schooling, her business and her finger print experience was superior to Miss Sullender's, but she was given 88 per cent. for experience.

Among the faults and errors which were specified by witnesses in addition to those above mentioned, were the disarrangement of the filing case, which trapped unsuspecting candidates, a shortness of time allowed for certain matters, the cutting down of some of the time allowances, by delays in the distribution of papers, interference by monitors, the failure of some candidates to receive cards which were required for some of the work, discrimination against those candidates who had been instructed in a certain school, concerning which Dr. DeForrest made disparaging remarks during the examination in the presence of candidates. For a long time the local commission attempted to sustain the examination, cross-examining the witnesses sharply and at length introducing the testimony of their own examiners; but finally they reversed the position which they had taken in rejecting the protest above referred to and cancelled the examination and the list which had resulted from it, notwithstanding the fact that the great majority of individual candidates who had appealed were rejected on their second examinations and that they had turned down the protest.

Referring to the counting of ridges in a finger print as an eyesight test above mentioned, Dr. DeForrest testified (page 704) that the "candidates were allowed to use a microscope or not as they pleased." They were also allowed to use a pointer if they desired, so it is evident that it was not a real test of eye-sight. Referring to the crowding for time, even Miss Sullender, who came out first and had an advantageous place in the room, admitted that she was rushed (page 815).

Examination for Statistician in Educational Department

President Moscowitz testified (page 6532) that it was his "special duty to supervise the work of the examiners." In the examination for Statistician in the Educational Department, Dr. Moscowitz appointed as special examiners, Professor E. L. Thorndike and Dr. L. P. Ayres. The result of the examination was that a Mr. Buckingham who was a student of and assistant to Professor Thorndike passed at the head of the list and was appointed to the position at a salary of $4,000; that a Mr. Clark whose application was endorsed by Dr. Ayres as a voucher, came out second on the list and that a Mr. Kelly, whose application was endorsed by Professor Thorndike as a voucher, came out third. Professor Thorndike was also voucher for Mr. Buckingham. Of the thirty-four candidates who were rejected on their experience sheets, *not one* of them had the endorsement of either Professor Thorndike or Dr. Ayres. Of the ten candidates who passed the experience test but failed in the written examination, only one had the endorsement of either Professor Thorndike or Dr. Ayres, and he was a Mr. Kavanagh, an employee of the Municipal Civil Service Commission, who was endorsed by Dr. Ayres but who could not pass the questions.

Mr. G. P. Watkins, assistant chief statistician in the Public Service Commission, failed in the final examination. He testified that he called on President Moscowitz on May 13, 1914, (the day the eligible list was promulgated). His testimony included the following (page 5600):

> "Q. You called his attention to the fact at that time that Mr. Buckingham was a pupil of Professor Thorndike? A. I did, yes, and also to the fact that he was evidently a personal friend of Mr. Ayres.
>
> *   *   *   *   *   *   *
>
> I am sure that I mentioned that because when I saw him I told him that the first knowledge I had that Mr. Ayres had anything to do with the examination, was through a remark

of Mr. Buckingham that Mr. Ayres and Professor Thorndike, that they were rating the papers and would probably have it done in a few weeks and were making good progress, something to that effect."

He gave similar testimony of information received that Mr. Ayres had stated a third person had been "jacked up" and said he gave the name of the person to Dr. Moscowitz, who did not ask that she be brought to him to confirm the information. It appears that at the very time that Mr. Watkins says he had a conversation with Dr. Moscowitz, the eligible lists were out and President Moscowitz did not refer to the fact. The witness said that Dr. Moscowitz seemed excited that there should be what he called a "leak." The witness went on to say:

> "After making all the elaborate preparations and pains that they had taken to prevent the identification of the papers by the examiners, the essential fact had not been taken into consideration that the examiners were well acquainted with a number of the people taking the examination and would identify a lot of papers or particular paper from the handwriting of the paper and under those circumstances I consider that the precautions taken at the examination room to detach the name of the writer of the paper from the paper and that the paper be labelled only by number and so forth was a farce and a fraud."

He said that he knew that in the case of Mr. Buckingham he was a favorite student of Professor Thorndike. The witness testified that he had been a public school teacher, had taught two years in Trinity College and two years in Cornell on Economics and Statistics. He testified that Professor Thorndike had developed a rather peculiar method in statistics and that, of course, his students would be trained in that sort of statistics. Mr. Buckingham, being asked whether he had practical experience as a statistician before he took the position, testified that he had worked with Dr. Thorndike in some of his investigations of schools, and had written a book on the matter of education measurements which was largely statistical in its character. He said he had told Professor Thorndike that he was taking the examination.

A letter was read in evidence from Mr. Kavanagh, above mentioned, who passed on experience but failed in the written test, endorsing the examination as a " noteworthy example of the efficiency of the merit system." Others wrote in criticism and condemnation of it. Miss Ida M. Metcalf employed as statistician on school matters in the finance department was rejected on her experience sheet though she had three college degrees, had taught public and private school most of her life and had been statistician in the department of finance over two years. She testified that her work during the last two years had been entirely on civic problems, so that she believed she had the requisite qualifications for the privilege of entering the written examination (page 5779). Another candidate, Frank L. Van Cleef, rejected on his experience paper, testified that he had taught in the University of Wisconsin and the University of Cornell for six years; that he had the degree of Bachelor of Arts from Oberlin College and from Cornell University and the degree of Doctor of Philosophy from Bonn University, Germany. He said (page 5785):

> " I am convinced my qualifications for a position in educational employment (particularly in higher mathematics) and experience in matters pertaining to statistical work are at least equal to those of the two candidates who were high enough to make them eligible for the examination."

The percentage marks received by the candidates who head the eligible list of three are Burdette R. Buckingham, 82 per cent., Earle Clark, 78 per cent. and Frederick J. Kelly, 75.51 per cent. There is an implied rule among civil service examiners that when candidates in a particular examination are few in number and any are known to them, that the examiners will not serve in the examination. President Moscowitz testified that he was informed by Professor Thorndike that he was acquainted with some of the candidates, and it was apparent that both Professor Thorndike and Dr. Ayres vouched for some of the very candidates they were expected to examine, and he said that it was entirely satisfactory to him and that he was *proud of the examination.* (Page 5603,)

We are of the opinion that the conduct of this examination was reprehensible, an injury to the merit system and calculated to produce distrust of the administration of the Civil Service Law.

Additional Cases of Unfair or Faulty Examinations

A number of complaints of unfair examinations in individual cases were made of which we select two illustrations. As an example: Edward T. Ernst and Thomas M. Wood were candidates in the examination for electrician (pages 2770–3273). These two papers were compared and it was found that Mr. Ernst was marked 50 per cent. for experience and Mr. Wood 83 per cent. On the expressed opinion of Mr. Saxton, Chief Examiner of the State Commission, to the effect that the difference in values was not sustained on examination of the papers, Commissioner Keogh's attention was called to the situation, but no explanation of it was made. Of course, it is difficult to sustain criticisms of this kind when the matters depend upon the individual judgment of the examiners, and perhaps such things are bound to occur, but in our opinion the complaint of Mr. Ernst was well-founded and is typical of a class of people who feel they have poor chances of success in the examinations. Mr. Ernst has had sixteen years of practical experience as electrician.

Another case that may be used as an illustration is that of Mr. Van Wert who was a candidate in the examination for salaries and grades examiner. Mr. Van Wert was examined June 2, 1914, and was rejected on a mark of 59 per cent. He was examined in a provisional examination, noncompetitive. He was examined again on June 26, 1914, and passed on a rating of 70 per cent. It appears (page 4329) that such re-examinations are given with considerable frequency. The examiner who rated the papers declined to express an approval of the policy of such re-examinations. Mr. Belcher, secretary to the municipal commission, stated (page 4332) that there is a rule against the practice, but that the commission may waive it. The rule in question is paragraph 12 of Rule 7, which provides that a candidate for a noncompetitive position shall not be re-examined within nine months of a failure unless for reasons stated in the resolution, that the provision be waived by the commission with relation to all candidates who fail, but not to any individual. An inspection of the ratings showed that on the first examination Van Wert was rated 90 on experience, but on the second, 80; on the first examination, 80 on education, but on the second, 75,—that on his first examination the ratings on questions were: 80, 40, 0, 70, 0, 0, 90 and that on the second examination with the five questions he was rated on them: 60, 70, 30, 70, 80.

In the case of Anthony P. Ludden, the municipal commission ignored the judgment of its examiners and ordered that Mr. Ludden be marked qualified as a noncompetitive appointee for a $4,000 position after he had *failed* on his examination; and President Moscowitz *defended* the order. Mr. Ludden was secretary of the market committee of the board of estimate. He was appointed temporarily under Rule 12, paragraph 4 on July 15, 1914. His payroll was passed on special certification pending the result of a noncompetitive examination under Rule 12, paragraph 3. That examination was held on September 10, 1914, and Mr. Ludden received a mark of 40 per cent. for experience which disqualified him for the position. Under Rule 12, paragraph 4, Mr. Ludden could hold his temporary position without examination no longer than thirty days. His period of temporary service extended from July 15th to September 10, 1914. Mr. Ludden appealed from the decision of the examiners in the noncompetitive examination and his appeal was rejected by Special Examiner Cyrus C. Miller and by Chief Examiner Ireland. Mr. Miller wrote:

> "On the face of the statements made in the appeal by Mr. Ludden he was engaged from March, 1909, until October 13, 1913, in the Customs Service of the United States making inquiries into certain affairs of the Customs Department. The scope and importance of these inquiries do not appear not does it appear that they had any relation to affairs of civic importance beyond any business of the Customs Service. An auditor of any railroad or steamship office might do the same work but it would not be called of civic importance. An affair which touches directly the civic life of the City and State or the United States would be of civic importance, but

the mere routine business of a department, any one of them, would not be of civic importance. It appears that Mr. Ludden was employed in the Bureau of one of the departments of the United States Government doing the routine work of that Bureau. *He has not shown experience in matters of civic importance.*"

Mr. Ludden requested a reconsideration of his appeal and on reconsideration he was again rejected by the examiners. On the second rejection of Mr. Ludden, Mr. Miller wrote (on November 28, 1914):

" The theory of the Civil Service Law is that all employees of the City shall be appointed for merit and upon competitive examinations. *Any exception to this rule is made only when the appointee has exceptional knowledge and ability for a particular place. It does not comply with the spirit of the law when a person lacking such qualifications is given an exempt position and thereafter acquires his knowledge of the duties of the place at the public expense.* It is quite evident that the appointee in this case has no special qualifications which entitle him to be an exception to the rule. However, the propriety of his original appointment or of his retention on payroll after his application for examination had been denied several times by the examiners *is something for which the examiners are not responsible.* * * * My attention has been called to the concluding paragraph of the advertisement in the City Record. * * * 'Candidates must submit evidence of an extended experience in the management of markets or extended purchase or handling of food stuffs or that they have made an extended practical study of the problems with which this Committee will have to deal.' It is urged on behalf of Mr. Ludden that he can qualify under the provision of having made an extended practical study of the problems with which this Committee will have to deal. *This paragraph is of recent date and was not in existence when the application was denied by the examiners.* The record shows that Mr. Ludden has acted as Secretary for a Market Committee organized by the President of the Bor-

> ough of Manhattan during part of the year 1914. The labors of this Market Committee have been directed chiefly towards the establishment of better markets in the City of New York. Such work embraces but a small part of the problems of marketing with which the City of New York is confronted through chiefly railroad and shipping and retail distribution problems which have little to do with the question of open markets. *I am unable to see that the employment of the applicant in such work for a portion of the year* 1914 *is of such a character as to entitle him to an examination for a position requiring the payment by the City of* $4,000 *for special knowledge."*

Mr. Ludden's rating of 70 *per cent. qualifying him for the position, pending a competitive examination was directed by the Commission itself at a meeting on December* 3, 1914, and was stated by the secretary of the Municipal Civil Service Commission to have been taken after consideration of the experience shown in the federal service and as secretary of the citizens' committee on markets. Mr. Ludden said he volunteered his services as such secretary in February, 1914, he had just begun the practice of law in New York city (October, 1913), having been an investigator for the customs department during the preceding four and one-half years. He had served as secretary of the market committee from February until July 15th, when he was appointed temporarily to the position at the salary mentioned. His payroll was passed on special certification pending the result of the non-competitive examination given under Rule 12, paragraph 3 on September 10th. It was not until December 3d that he was actually rerated *by order of the Commission in their opposition to the judgment of its examiners and was given the passing mark of* 70 *per cent.* He had exceeded the thirty-day limit of his appointment by twenty-five days and as a result of his failure to pass the non-competitive examination and of the subsequent arbitrary action of the Commission itself he was permitted to remain in office at the rate of $4,000 a year for nearly three months additional. *Mr. Ludden could not have been paid for his temporary services until he had qualified in the noncompetitive examination* *and he testified that he received his first payment, $666, on December 7th, four days after the Municipal Commission ordered him qualified.* (Page 3999).

Mr. Ludden is still in office. President Moscowitz commended the examiner, Mr. Miller, as one of the best men he could find. (Page 4012.) Assistant Chief Examiner Fuld, in a report dated December 3, 1914, addressed to President Moscowitz, said:

> " In my opinion Mr. Ludden's services as secretary to this committee from February to July, during which period he devoted about an hour a day to the duties of his position, *do not* constitute such ' extended practical study of the problems with which this committee will have to deal ' as is required by the printed advertisement of the Civil Service Commission of candidates in competitive examination for this position."

The Case of Kerner Easton

Mr. Easton was exempted from examination for the position as secretary of the committee on port and terminal facilities of the board of estimate and apportionment and was appointed at $5,000 a year under Rule 12, paragraph 5. The spirit and purpose of civil service were flagrantly violated. Mr. Easton had no exceptional qualifications whatever for the position and his exemption is an injustice to those who might compete for the place. Mr. Easton is a young man of social position and was engaged in the practice of law prior to his appointment. Mr. Easton testified that Dock Commissioner Smith had stated that he was one of the " most available and one of the most desirable candidates " before the committee at that time; that for two or three months prior to his appointment he familiarized himself with " all the undertakings of the board of estimate for six years in the matter of port improvements and examined reports in connection with South Brooklyn and became familiar with the layout and general plans," and that he familiarized himself with those matters to qualify for the position. (Page 5897.) He said he did this so that when he appeared before the committee he would not be talking at random and would know what he was talking about, and that for two or three months he pursued the information diligently.

In paragraph 5 of Rule 12, under which Mr. Easton was appointed without competition, it is provided that:

> "When there is a vacancy in any position in the competitive class demanding peculiar and *exceptional* qualifications of a *scientific, professional or educational character and upon satisfactory evidence and several specified reasons competition in such special case is not practicable* and that the position can best be filled by the selection of some disinterested person of high and recognized attainments and such qualities, that the commissioner may suspend the provisions of the rule requiring competition in such case, but no such suspension shall be general in its application to such position."

Mr. Easton's testimony shows conclusively that his selection as secretary of the committee on port and terminal facilities without competitive examination was *not contemplated* under this provision of the civil service rules. Mr. Easton stated (page 5901) that he gathered information during the two or three months preceding his appointment and following the filing of his application, by reading reports relative to terminal matters in order to qualify for the position. The attitude of the Civil Service Reform Association may be seen in the statement of Secretary Keyes opposing the exemption of Mr. Easton (page 5905). He emphasizes the fact that satisfactory evidence was not submitted to show that competition for the position was not practicable. *The Municipal Commission yielded to the desire of the dock commissioner, expressed orally before them in behalf of his personal choice.* Undoubtedly this is one of the cases referred to by Commissioner Keogh in his testimony. A number of similar cases will be exhibited elsewhere in this report.

Department of Public Works

The departments of public works are under the jurisdiction of the borough presidents, with bureau of sewers, bureau of highways, bureau of design and survey, chief engineer's office, etc.

Our attention was directed to the department of public works in the borough of Manhattan, controlled by Commissioner E. V. Frothingham, with engineers and bureau heads, all holding over from a former administration. We found in said borough, the only one we had time to examine, serious violations of the Civil Service Law. These violations were mainly these: The consulting engineer, E. P. Goodrich, appointed without examination under section 386 of the charter, *does not act as consulting engineer in the true sense of the term, but is the practical directing and executive engineering head of the department.* There also is an assistant consulting engineer, Mr. Schaeffer, though the charter allows only *one* consulting engineer. Mr. Goodrich is also consulting engineer of the court house board. He receives $7,200 a year from the borough of Manhattan and $7,500 a year from the court house board. Until recently he has been consulting engineer of other cities, some of them being on the Pacific coast, and he conducts a private engineering business, does the work for the inebriety board, and is the practical head of the sewer plan commission, which is planning new sewers in Manhattan estimated to cost from fifty to one hundred million dollars. Charles E. Gregory, chief engineer of sewers, and very closely associated with Mr. Goodrich, is secretary of said sewer plan commission, which place and others he holds at Mr. Goodrich's suggestion.

Mr. Goodrich's executive control, shown by his own testimony and by that of Engineer Gardiner, has been effected largely by the selection of engineers of his personal acquaintance to hold important posts, and exempting them from competitive examinations through resolutions of the Municipal Commission passed without hesitation under the system criticized by Commissioner Keogh, as before stated. He said he was not concerned about the law; he wanted to put the men he wanted to the work he wanted done.

In bureaus cliques of men have secured control by ignoring the plain provisions of the Civil Service Law; men in these cliques often holding positions in which their work is entirely inappropriate to their civil service titles. In this situation, of gravest import from the standpoint of civil service principles, the payrolls have been made out and certified *falsely,* both by the representatives of the department and the employees of the Municipal

Civil Service Commission, *after offending payrolls were produced and exhibited to the commissioners, their secretary and their counsel. The borough president learning of some of these conditions has appointed a new deputy commissioner to succeed the one who certified most of the offending payrolls, and has appointed a new engineer in charge of the bureau of highways to supersede the engineer in charge, who, though appointed as an " expert " in paving, was so inexperienced in the paving required in New York city that previously to his coming to the city he had not laid a yard of asphalt, wood-block or granite pavement* (though in Panama, from whence he came, he had laid considerable macadam and brick pavement). A " clerk " who was acting as chief of the bureau of maintenance of sewers has gone to another department to work truly as a clerk, and two sewer cleaners, who assisted him in the office, have been sent out into the field to clean sewers. These changes have occurred within about a month, and since the facts were publicly developed by this investigation. This commission makes no reflection whatever on the borough president, who alone has acted, while the Municipal Civil Service Commission has stood supine — inactive — still passing the payrolls untruly certified.

Attention will now be directed to certain engineers who were brought into the department without examination, or competition, under said rule 12, on the ground of " peculiar and exceptional qualifications of a scientific, professional, or educational character " and that the persons designated are of " high and recognized attainments."

These men went over the heads of good, experienced engineers, acquainted with New York city problems, some of whom had grown gray in the city's service.

Henry W. Durham (p. 5303) was appointed chief engineer of highways, an exempt position, with salary of $5,000. He worked for the Panama Canal Commission in charge of the waterworks, sewers, streets, roads and pavements in the city of Panama. As stated above, he had *no* experience in the pavements required in New York city, though for four years he was assistant engineer on the subway construction. Since he has been chief engineer, a hundred miles of pavement have been laid in Manhattan borough, much of which is wood-block in which he had no experience (and the specifications for which have been shown to be very technical and subject to great suspicion). Mr. Durham was recently superseded by a new appointee of the borough president.

John C. Wolfe (pages 2641, 2645 and 5206) was an assistant engineer in the Public Service Commission, and was acquainted with Mr. Goodrich, at whose request, in 1910, he came over into the service of the Borough of Manhattan, Department of Public Works, without an examination. He claimed that his work for the Public Service Commission gave him a knowledge of sewer conditions and he claimed to have done some sewer work at the Bush Terminal Stores, in Brooklyn, under Mr. Goodrich, who had charge of the work (and who is related to Mr. Bush). Some time after he was placed in the city's service, he took a *promotion* examination. On promotion examination efficiency marks count most, and these are given by the head of the bureau in which the man works. Mr. Wolfe having entered the service without examination on the ground of a superior knowledge of *sewers,* and having been assigned to Mr. Goodrich's office, was set to work on building the *asphalt repair plant* in Manhattan, and when that uncertain affair was finished, he was assigned to the *superintendency of the vast Municipal Building*—though he had never had any experience in the management of a great office building—and he still holds that responsible position *without special qualification, and with no examination of candidates for that place.* Upon being pressed (p. 5208) he said, "I really don't know what the special ability I was exempted for was."

The request for the exemption of Mr. Wolfe and of Mr. Appleby and Mr. Sullivan was made by the borough president in September, 1910, on the ground that Mr. Goodrich wished to organize a new bureau *of subway engineering and traffic observation* and desired to appoint these *three men* because of their peculiar fitness, etc.

Henry D. Appleby (pp. 2662, 2677) came into the department of public works with a salary of $3,000, without examination, and *never has taken an examination.* His salary has been increased to $3,500. He now has charge of the Bureau of Design and Survey, though at first he was assistant to Mr. Goodrich. His first work was in the analysis of subway traffic, and in traffic regulations, and in indexing and filing maps and records of the department. He claimed that he came without examination as an "expert" in knowledge of the designing of subways, in standardization methods, and in control of men. He said he started to work inside of a month after his appointment *in making a new method of filing and indexing maps, though he had never before done that sort of work* (p. 2667). He was asked what were the peculiar scientific qualifications he had for getting his position without examination (p. 2888). He evaded the question and finally said the first peculiar and scientific thing he did was to analyze the subway traffic — which he explained as the drawing of a topographical chart with a sheer curve showing the fluctuations of traffic to determine the "average haul" of passengers. This was made up *from the records* of the Interborough Company and the Public Service Commission. Being further pressed (p. 2678) he said, "Well, I cannot tell you what qualifications the people who appointed me considered I had." Then he proceeded to say he had a general knowledge of engineering covering sixteen years, but he wouldn't say he was the only man who had such experience. He said probably there were others who could do the same things that he, Wolfe and Sullivan did (p. 2680). He was simply invited to come in and he went in the way it opened (p. 2684).

John F. Sullivan (p. 2693) came from the Public Service Commission into the Department of Public Works and into Mr. Goodrich's office at a salary of $2,100 *without examination.* He was transferred to the Board of Estimate, where he is receiving $5,000, at the request of Tilden Adamson, director of the Bureau of Contract Supervision. Mr. Sullivan had a promotion examination in 1911. *Nobody was examined but himself* (p. 2695). He *had increases of salary from* $2,400 *to* $5,000 *without any other examination and without any request.* The most important work he has been engaged upon is *the New York Central Railroad track plan on Eleventh Avenue.*

John H. Weinberger (p. 2636), an assistant engineer, was transferred from the Borough of Queens to the Bureau of Sewers in Manhattan, where he was appointed to a vacancy as the first assistant engineer, over the head of a veteran engineer, Norman B. Gardiner, to whom the place had been promised by the engineer in charge, who had the appointing power. His qualifications for sewer work were inferior to those of Mr. Gardiner, and his coming over into the Manhattan office blocked the opportunity for promotion that seemed to have come to a faithful and experienced engineer.

The responsibility of Charles E. Gregory, chief engineer of sewers, for conditions herein described, and his dependence upon Mr. Goodrich will be seen in his testimony (pages 2571, 2600, 2628, 2640, 6392), and the responsibility of Commissioner Frothingham will appear in his testimony (p. 1317, etc.) and in the general record.

On March 26, 1914, the president of the Municipal Civil Service Commission received a letter charging that various employees were doing work inappropriate to their titles in the Sewer Bureau, and specifying fourteen names, including T. J. McCarthy, sewer cleaner, doing clerical work; J. A. Hartnedy, clerk, acting as superintendent of the cleaning division; Joseph Frank, transitman in charge of permits (for street openings); H. Dreyfus, telephone operator, acting as elevator dispatcher (in Municipal Building), and others.

Examiner Fuld investigated and rendered a report finding that a number of the specifications were true and recommending that the titles of four men should be changed, that four other men should be assigned to appropriate duties, and he advised promotion examinations for four others. Among these were Joseph Frank, transitman at present performing the duties of chief of the permit division or assistant engineer (he is still doing the same work under the same title), and John A. C. Hartnedy, who was performing the duties of maintenance manager or superintendent of sewer cleaning. (He continued under the same title doing the same work until he was transferred as clerk to the commissioners of accounts, January 1, 1915.) He reported that examinations be advised for Thomas J. McCarthy, sewer cleaner, doing the work of foreman of sewer cleaners, and O. J. Swenson, inspector, doing the work of chief inspector or supervising inspector. He advised that the services of *William James Smith,* emergency bookkeeper doing clerical work be dispensed with, and that an inquiry be made whether the work done by Mr. Smith was such as to require special training and experience as a bookkeeper.

On June 5, 1914, a letter was received by President Moscowitz from the Preferred List Clerk's Association, calling attention to the continuance of said conditions. It declared that a Stephen Kelly (civil service clerk) had managed to secure the continuance of his friends in their places to the detriment of the members of the Preferred List Clerks whose chances of certification would expire. It called attention to sewer cleaners still performing clerical work, and a clerk (Hartnedy) supervising the maintenance force. Said letter contained a list of nine specific violations of law in continuance, including Hartnedy, Clifford, McCarthy, Swenson, Frank and Berrigan, hereinafter referred to. Examiner Fuld submitted another report, in which he found matters reflecting severely upon sewer cleaner McCarthy. He said that on April 10, 1914, he had reported that said McCarthy was performing work inappropriate to his title and that he had applied for promotion to foreman of sewer cleaners, and suggested that the derogatory facts be submitted to McCarthy's superiors.

Stephen Kelly is the civil service clerk of the Public Works Department, and is expected to keep that department and its employees straight in all civil service matters. Mr. William J. Smith is his old friend and associate. Through his knowledge of vacancies, rules and opportunities, he was able to keep Mr. Smith on the payroll for two years without competitive examination and he is still there, though Smith is *no* "expert" in anything—just a plain bookkeeper.

In August, 1912, Smith was appointed an inspector at $1,200 a year, held the position one month and failed on a noncompetitive examination. He then became an axeman at $900 a year, under temporary appointment, which he managed to continue for a year, checking inspectors' reports of pavement conditions. He never carried an axe or went out with a party. *He passed a competitive examination for axeman, and not being appointed took a noncompetitive examination because he had secured the appointment.* As a noncompetitive axeman, he worked a year under a transitman named Joseph Frank, who had charge in the office of the bureau of permits (mentioned above). He passed from axeman to bookkeeper, and under that title he remains acting as a clerk in the bureau of permits. As a bookkeeper he checks paving reports, *the same as he did when he was an axeman.* He has one book showing refunds, containing about 400 pages. His *temporary* appointment as a bookkeeper has run a *year,* at $1,500 salary. He passed directly from $900 to $1,500 *without any change of duties.*

President Moscowitz (p. 1415) said that the bookkeeper's examination had been delayed.

John A. Hartnedy has been a clerk since 1906, and was in the sewer bureau from 1910 to January 1, 1915, when he was transferred to the Commissioner of Accounts. Mr. Hartnedy was absent from his position for long stretches of time on sick leave; nevertheless he maintained a close hold upon the important bureau of maintenance of sewers, and was its active and actual head, working through others when he was absent. He made and kept the efficiency ratings of the men assigned to his bureau, ratings which counted heavily for or against promotion. This mere clerk did not simply assume the functions of direction and control,— but he was secured in his anomalous position by direct action of the Chief Engineer, and with the recognition of the so-called bureau of efficiency. It is inconceivable that the commissioner and his deputy did not know of the illegal situation, yet his payroll was regularly certified by the deputy commissioner, Mr. Patterson, with the statement that he as clerk *had not performed duties inappropriate to his title.* The letters received by President Moscowitz mentioned Mr. Hartnedy and his violation of law in detail, and the report of Examiner Fuld *confirmed* it, yet *the municipal civil service commission passed his pay on those untruthful certificates down to the day of his transfer, January* 1, 1915.

The responsibility of Chief Engineer Gregory for this condition is evidenced by his own writings, several of which appear in the record (pp. 2602–5). On March 30, 1914, he wrote a letter to eleven bricklayers and foremen directing them to accept all orders and instructions from Mr. Hartnedy, and directing them to obey him in letter and in spirit as to the orders which he might issue from time to time. Letters written to the general inspector and general foreman, and to an assistant foreman, stated that the repair forces, field and office, must report to Mr. Hartnedy and be under his jurisdiction, and that the *general foreman* must turn over to him all papers and records relating to the repairs division. At the same time the general foreman, William Klein, was relieved of a large part of his duties, which were transferred to Jeremiah Lynch, *a mason,* who became the practical general inspector, while William Klein's duties were so changed as to make him a general foreman in name only.

That Mr. Hartnedy took the full value of this designation by the chief engineer appears not so clearly in his testimony as in his letters. His letter books were put in evidence, and showed him issuing written orders on all kinds of executive matters to all persons in the bureau, and making regular reports of the operations of the bureau, which with men, officers, carts, wagons and tools, did the physical work of maintaining sewers. He signed usually as "Chief of the Bureau of Maintenance." (See extracts from Hartnedy's letter books, pages 6543–4 and 5937.) Mr. Hartnedy's *unusual* and remarkable absences from duty for sickness appear in the record (p. 952).

Thomas F. McCarthy (p. 956, etc.), a sewer cleaner mentioned above, was an important factor in Mr. Hartnedy's clique bureau and holds the same post, though Hartnedy is gone. He is an effective force in the rating and handling of the men in that bureau. In 1911 sewer cleaner McCarthy was transferred from the field to Mr. Hartnedy's office (p. 957), and he attended to the business of the office done by telephone, such as complaints of sewer flooding and the like. He hands out the work to the sewer gangs, maps out their work, and handles the inspectors' reports under Mr. Hartnedy. Mr. Hartnedy told him he was trying to have a title made for him that would fit his work. In the fall of 1914 Mr. McCarthy did take a promotion examination for foreman of sewer cleaners and passed. It is very doubtful whether that title includes the work he is doing.

This bureau of sewers was organized with its personnel, by the efficiency bureau of the commissioner of accounts office, of which Mr. Welton is the head (pp. 967–8).

In October, 1914, Mr. McCarthy testified that sewer cleaner Thomas Roach had been in the office acting as a messenger for a year. Engineer Gregory testified to the same fact (p. 6393). A foreman named Cathie was acting as general foreman. Mr. McCarthy, being fresh from the physical examination for foreman of sewer cleaners, was asked about it. He declared that there was *no* examination of feet, legs, heart, lungs or body; no inquiry for disease, but only the dumb-bell test and the eye card test. He said he was asked by the examiner to read the first line on the card (20 feet away) and that he did so easily and readily;— it was the word EXAMINATION. When he repeated it, he said the examiner told him it was all right. The medical examiner produced the medical record which showed he had been marked *perfect* for the slip number one which was some way down the board and showed the letters T L O T D E X C, a jumble of small letters (pages 999–100, 970–6, etc). He thought all the candidates were allowed to read the word "examination" because as a class they have poor eyes; it was an easy test (pages 1001–3). He said the work (for which so slight a physical examination was given), was underground and dangerous, men sometimes being overcome by gases, that they needed good hearts, and that there was strain on the eyes,— that they have to be on their feet all the time. (No examination for flat foot or varicose veins, though such examination was required for finger print examiners.)

Mr. McCarthy was all the time number two on the eligible list for assistant foreman, but a veteran named Hamill was first on the list so it was *not used.* Hamill is a laborer acting as a watchman (p. 987). The witness specified Hayes, Hogan and Moynihan as men who were acting as foremen, though *not foremen,* and said that Darragh, whose title is general foreman, is simply in charge of the yard, while Foreman Cathie does the work which legally devolves on Darragh.

Mr. McCarthy was not promoted to be foreman of sewer cleaners until December 21, 1914, *and yet he remained as a sewer cleaner in the office ordering and directing other sewer cleaners and supervising their work, and doing all the work under Mr. Hartnedy that had been complained of in March,* 1914, *and reported by examiner Fuld at or about that time to President Moskowitz as a clear violation of the Civil Service Law, while his superiors and the Municipal Civil Service Commission certified his payroll on false certificates.*

With a bureau of maintenance organized and operated in defiance of law, by the famous "efficiency bureau," and all the authorities ignoring the protests of the preferred clerks, who were discriminated against by this illegal action, *it cannot be wondered at that the men in the department of sewers who are not in the favored circles are disgusted with civil service and look upon it not as a protection for honest workers, but as a device for the exercise of pull and privilege. That distrust is not limited to the ranks, but goes into the higher positions.*

Ralph Lewis is a transitman (p. 5228). As a transitman he was raised from $1,500 to $1,800 on a temporary promotion. He took a promotion examination for a higher grade and failed and about the same time took an examination for assistant engineer and passed, number one, but has not been appointed. Failing to pass the examination in the higher grade of transitman, which he held temporarily, his salary fell back to $1,500, but he made no refund of the additional money drawn at higher rate. Now as a transitman in an inferior grade, he has charge of the highway division of the bureau of design and survey, supervising the work of that division. It is purely an engineer's position (p. 2231). For about seven months he thus has been doing an engineer's work. Other persons in the department are doing the same kind of work, but they are engineers — he specified their names. Mr. Lewis superseded an engineer named Charles Levy who was demoted and placed under him, with a salary of $2,100 — $300 *more* than Mr. Lewis now is receiving. He put the responsibility for the situation on Engineer Appleby, which is quite natural considering the way that Mr. Appleby came into the department (p. 5232). Mr. Lewis' regular appointment as engineer is blocked by a preferred list of 40 engineers laid off from other departments. If he were not doing the work under his title of transitman, one of those laid-off engineers would get the position — so they conspire to nullify the law and violate its spirit, in the interest of Lewis, and they are allowed to do it.

Otto J. Swenson (p. 5235), referred to in the complaints above mentioned, is an inspector, but he is doing the work of an engineer, having supervision of the record division of the smooth-pavement maintenance division, and of the passing of plant-materials and supplies. He is general assistant to the chief engineer and investigating complaints. He is making computations for the annual report, showing different costs, and has made computation of the strengths of granite, etc. He is a graduate engineer, and exercises his engineering knowledge in his work (p. 5236). He admits that it is engineering work. His salary is $2,250 a year, but he remains an inspector, and has done so since 1912. He specifies four engineers who are doing the same kind of work as his — their salaries varying from $2,100 to *$4,000. He failed in two examinations for assistant engineer* (page 5239).

Charles C. Jabureck (p. 5315) is an assistant engineer. He started as a draftsman in the department of public works in 1911, having been appointed after examination for that position which he took while holding the position of civil engineer in the Public Service Commission. In 1914 he was promoted to assistant engineer after a promotion examination, and has been increased in salary. He is an assistant to Mr. Appleby. Careful examination failed to reveal the doing of real engineering work, except the construction of two sheds, which occupied relatively but a small part of his time.

Michael J. Berrigan (p. 5327) is an inspector of complaints by title, but is actually a clerk, performing clerical duties and doing little if any inspecting. He was included in the original complaint mentioned above.

Joseph Frank (p. 5331), also mentioned in said complaints, has already been described as the transitman, who has charge of the permit division in the general office.

Patrick Clifford (p. 5560) is a foreman who did clerical work under Mr. Hartnedy until he was put out in the field, January 1, 1915. He was mentioned in the old complaints.

William McGillick (p. 5407) is a sewer cleaner who does night duty attending the telephone and writing reports.

Harold C. Todd (p. 2164) has the title of supervising inspector but he has charge of fifty-nine public buildings (except the Municipal Building which is in Mr. Wolfe's care). He selects, appoints, discharges the employees, and attends to the maintenance and operation of the buildings. His present title was obtained in August, 1914; before that it was "confidential inspector." He entered the city's service February 1, 1911, under that title at $1,800 a year, exempted from examination. His position as supervising inspector at $3,000 a year, in charge of said buildings was also provisional and without competitive examination, though an examination for permanent appointment has been called.

This gentleman's experience in the management of buildings, to enable him to compete with others for the permanent appointment, *is that which he has gained in his temporary and provisional appointments,* for he did not graduate from Columbia University until June, 1910. His present duties differ from those which he performed as "confidential inspector" (exempt) only in that they increased as he assumed more authority — so he says: Mr. Todd by steady assumption of authority has become the practical czar of the public buildings; his word is law. Mr. Coudert was led to remark: "Pretty nice young men we turn out of Columbia * * * It's hard to beat them. You have to get up early to get ahead of a Columbia young man;" which doubtless is true if he makes the right connections.

Jeremiah Lynch (pp. 906 and 2065, etc.): The story of Mr. Lynch is an interesting one. He was a mason, but instead of working under his title, he acted as general foreman — supervising the work of masons and bricklayers and supervising the work of foremen masons and foremen bricklayers — indeed in the program of the "efficiency bureau," which put Mr. Hartnedy the clerk in as chief of the maintenance of sewers, with his friends as office assistants regardless of their titles and duties as sewer cleaners, etc., Jeremiah Lynch was put into the duties of the old general foreman, Mr. Klein, who was relegated to the backyard. This assumption of authority by Mr. Lynch over men of his own title and standing, and over bricklayers as well, caused much friction and the labor organizations intervened. During all this time while Mr. Lynch was doing the work of a general foreman under the express directions of clerk John A. Hartnedy acting as chief of maintenance, the officials of the department falsely certified the payrolls, to the effect that he was performing only the duties *appropriate to his title,* and was doing no other work, *and the municipal civil service commission was passing said payrolls.* The assigning of this mason to the important work described was *made with the knowledge and approval of Chief Engineer Gregory.*

On June 11, 1914, the Bricklayers' and Masons' International Union protested to the Municipal Civil Service Commission, and *no* relief being had, they protested again on October 31, 1914, the written protests following consideration of the matter in their regular meeting.

The protest informed the Municipal Commission that the procedure in Mr. Lynch's case was a "*peculiar manipulation of favoritism.*" It showed that in April, the work of repairing sewers which was in the hands of a practical mechanic, was put in the hands of an "efficiency clerk" who assumed the office title of Supervisor of Maintenance, though he knew nothing of bricklaying from a practical standpoint (meaning the clerk Hartnedy, *who was off duty a third of his time*). This clerk selected a stone mason (Mr. Lynch) to direct this brick work, *ignoring all bricklayers,* foremen bricklayers and foremen masons in the department. Matters became strained under the violation of law, and the clerk requested a promotion examination for his friend so that he might be made a foreman mason. This examination was formally requested by the Commission on April 20, 1914. The examination being for foreman mason it was limited to the three masons in the department and excluded the bricklayers, of whom there were many, for nearly all sewer work is of brick. On account of the protest of the Union, this scheme was dropped, and another examination was requested *in which bricklayers might compete.* This, however, was arranged for the bricklayers and only one stone mason (Lynch), for the other stone masons could get no application blanks (p. 1912). Again the Union protested, and on July 31, to meet the emergency, Commissioner Frothingham requested the Civil Service Commission to allow the masons to *change their titles to bricklayers,* which request was granted on August 12, 1914, and a practical test was ordered, *though an eligible list and preferred list were in existence.* After all these arrangements the examination was ordered for foreman bricklayer. The Union closed its protest with these words (p. 1914):

"We say plain and simple the most flagrant violations of the civil service law have been carried on." It asks "Why such flagrant abuses of the civil service laws are permitted at the behest of those desiring to place a favorite?" It asked the reason for the discrimination against the foreman mason in the bureau of sewers who also is legally eligible.

Mr. Lynch stated positively that clerk Hartnedy acted as superintendent and foreman and had full charge of the basin cleaning gangs — himself taking full charge of the work. (See the style of orders and letters issued by him, pages 5937 etc., 6543 etc.) He had seen the provision in the new budget for a new position of foreman of bricklayers — and hoped he would get it through the examination he has taken. We are informed that Mr. Lynch is still rated as a mason, and is still acting as general foreman.

Joseph J. Kletchka (p. 2832) was an engineer in the Department of Public Works for twenty years. In the early part of 1913, he was laid off by Chief Engineer of Sewers, Mr. Durham, on the ground that they were putting on high priced inspectors, and had too many engineers. The formal dismissal was based on alleged *lack of work.* However *there was more work than usual* and Kletchka was busy at that time. Mr. Kletchka protested on the ground that if some man had to go it should be a new-comer like Wolfe, Appleby or Sullivan. "Seeing that it was no use," he said, "I took my medicine."

Previous to his being laid off, Mr. Kletchka had condemned 190,000 *granite paving blocks not up to specifications, furnished by a contractor named Fitzgerald.* Mr. Kletchka now holds a responsible position in a private concern.

(Payrolls referring to some of the cases above mentioned were put in evidence — see pages 6550, 6617.)

John B. Wild (p. 5240) is an inspector in the department of public works. He was appointed, temporary, non-competitive, September 12, 1911, at $1,200 a year. He stayed so about a year and then became permanent through competitive examination. In New York city he inspected the laying of asphalt paving — his only previous employment in that line was for about eight months on and off, inspecting the laying of *macadam pavement* in Passaic county, New Jersey. He had been employed previously in the Rogers Locomotive Works, where he was a *mechanic* and became a *draftsman.* Just prior to coming into employment in New York city he was a *bookkeeper.*

He admitted that when he came into the service of New York city he had *no* expert knowledge of pavements.

In June he began to do special work for New York city, *inspecting the manufacture of wood blocks for paving,* being assigned to that work as an expert by *Engineer Sullivan* at $10 a day, and travelling expenses. This alleged "expert" in the manufacture of wood blocks for paving was absolutely *unqualified.* He admitted that all he knew of the subject was picked up in the American Creosoting Company's plant at Newark, *while he was inspecting their manufactured blocks for the city of New York.* This is one of the associated companies hereinafter mentioned, and his assignment to it was by Engineer Sullivan. He admitted that when he went there, he had no practical experience whatever — that nobody instructed him — all he learned he "picked up." He had no idea how Engineer Sullivan imagined he knew anything about it; he had no training in chemistry, and knew nothing of the oils, creosote, coal derivatives, etc., etc., or anything else connected with it (though highly technical knowledge of the treatment of wood in particular with special oils is required for proper inspection). He said: "Well, I knew in a rough way that there was a certain treatment given to wood, and was put in under pressure and that is all I know." The work in New Jersey was done under his regular salary as inspector of asphalt paving ($1,200 per year), and then he was sent to Indianapolis and to Norfolk at $10 a day and expenses and remained at those places for several months.

Wood-block paving has long been a subject of suspicion as to the meaning and purpose of specifications, and it has been charged for years that so-called *closed* specifications are devised and adopted by the engineers of various cities, in which there are clauses so worded *as to limit the oil substantially to that which is produced mainly by a great combination of related corporations operating throughout the nation.* The importance of competent and careful inspection is evident. Mr. Wild said that the engineers who selected him as an expert inspector, at expert's pay, were *Mr. Sullivan and Mr. Durham.* This being so, their action was *reprehensible.*

A. W. Dow, a chemist, is employed in the Borough of Bronx as an expert on asphalt, and was employed in the Borough of Manhattan as expert to instruct inspectors (of pavements). Two witnesses of standing and repute testified that he was known throughout the country as a *representative of the wood-paving trust and interests; one of them testifying that he admitted the receipt of money from one of said wood-paving companies for advocating the kind of specifications in the City of New York that favored its heavy oil.* Mr. Dow was asked to appear as a witness but preferred to attend an engineers' convention.

(The subject of wood-block paving in the City of New York is treated in an appendix to this report.)

Health Department

Unlicensed Physicians in Charge of City Hospitals — Unregistered Nurses Control Hospital Wards and Supervise the Work of Registered Nurses, and Civil Service Rules Generally Ignored in Health Department Hospitals.

Besides acknowledging under oath that he employs unlicensed and nonresident physicians to treat patients in the public hospitals, Dr. Robert J. Wilson, medical director of the health department, testified that nonregistered nurses were in charge of sick wards and were directing and supervising the work of graduate and registered nurses. He said that this condition was general in the institutions under his jurisdiction and he acknowledged that civil service *regulations were generally disregarded so far as the disposition of the hospital force is concerned.* The State Commission had received lengthy complaints about the civil service irregularities in the health department hospitals and asked Dr. Wilson about them. The doctor testified on November 25 and January 8, and each time his testimony disclosed flagrant disregard of civil service provisions. On January 8, 1915, Dr. Wilson admitted that Dr. Green, assistant resident physician at the Willard Parker Hospital, was unlicensed, and that Dr. Dixon, the resident physician, was a Canadian and not a citizen of the United States.

> "Q. (p. 5868) And still you continue employing him (Dr. Green)? A. Yes.
>
> "Q. Do you think it is a proper thing? A. I do not think it is an advisable thing."

Dr. Wilson acknowledged that Dr. Westmoreland, at Riverside Hospital, and Dr. Cannon, at Kingston Avenue Hospital, were *unlicensed physicians* in the employ of the health department.

Protest had been made to the municipal civil service commission about the fact that unregistered nurses were advanced in salary and were in authority over nurses registered in this State, and these complaints were repeated to the State Commission. The investigation disclosed the fact that at least six of the health department nurses in charge of wards, floors or hospitals, superintending the work of other nurses, were not registered and that *they were increased from* $600 *to* $720 *a year during the summer of* 1914. Dr. Wilson testified that he increased these nurses of his own volition; that he held an examination in which half the nurses (150) in the health department entered, and he formed his judgment on the result of the examination. The position of nurse is in the noncompetitive class, and there is a board of promotion for noncompetitive employees in the department whose actions are subject to the approval of the municipal civil service commission. This board, however, according to Dr. Wilson, had no responsibility whatever for the elevation of the unregistered nurses over those who are registered. Dr. Wilson testified that he was a member of the promotion board (p. 5889), that the board keeps the efficiency ratings of all noncompetitive employees, and the constitution and by-laws of the board were adopted by the municipal civil service commission as a "model" for all city departments (p. 5890). In spite of this fact, the civil service commission, through the promotion board, *had no control whatever over the promotions made and acknowledged by Dr. Wilson.*

Dr. Wilson was asked with reference to at least a score of employees in the hospitals under his jurisdiction and he acknowledged that in each case the civil service law was violated, the individual being engaged in other service than that indicated by the civil service title. In one case an orderly was serving as electrician; in another case a " laborer " was serving as laboratory assistant; orderlies were engaged as mechanics and laborers; hospital clerks do stenographic work; laborers serve as watchmen, attendants, painters, telephone operators and carpenters; and domestics serve as cooks, assistant cooks, chambermaids, seamstresses, attendants, helpers and *telephone operators* (p. 3582).

Dr. Wilson acknowledged that he was responsible for the distribution " of the labor of all of the employees " and that he signs all the payrolls of the hospitals.

Listening to the testimony of Anna Fennell, a domestic who has operated the telephone for seven years, he was asked:

> " Q. Do you certify that she works as a domestic when you sign the payroll? A. *I certainly do.* I wish to make an explanation on that whole thing."

Then he testified that he called the attention of the civil service commission to the fact that " domestics " worked in various other capacities and that the board of estimate declined to vote appropriations that he might employ persons according to their civil service designations. *Dr. Wilson testified that the board of estimate has consistently denied him money to employ telephone operators* to relieve the orderlies and domestics doing that work (p. 358). The testimony disclosed that domestics were paid the same amount as civil service telephone operators.

Dr. Wilson testified that he prepared the annual budget for all hospitals within the jurisdiction of the health department, that he increased his own salary in the tentative budget last summer from $3,000 to $6,000 and that it was passed at $5,000, and that the board of estimate declined to fill the position of lay superintendent at Otisville Sanitarium at $3,000 because of insufficient funds (p. 3576), though the institution has 585 patients and an examination for the position was held and list established. The position has been vacant since Jan. 1, 1914. Dr. Wilson testified that with the increase in salary his title was changed to medical director from superintendent though the duties *remained the same.*

Anna M. Gaynor, a clerk in the health department, testified (p. 3524), that she had her title changed from "hospital clerk" to clerk, making her eligible for third grade clerkship in any city department. The position of "hospital clerk" is noncompetitive and that of "clerk" is in the competitive class. She made application with other hospital clerks in the department for a change of title and the civil service commission by resolution in 1914, made the change in her favor (p. 3831). Dr. Wilson subsequently testified that the change requested by the other hospital clerks was denied *though each of them was as much entitled to the change as was Miss Gaynor* (p. 3570). One of the three other hospital clerks whose request was denied, had qualified through civil service examination, for the position of "hospital clerk" and was in charge of the storeroom at Willard Parker Hospital with a force of six clerks and laborers under him.

Besides the violations of the civil service law in the health department acknowledged by Dr. Wilson, the investigation disclosed that four physicians hold office and draw pay at the rate of $1,200 per year each, *without proper classification.* These physicians are Drs. Scouler, Weed, Stoney and Frick, each of whom conducts a clinic in some part of Brooklyn. The State Commission summoned Dr. Ambrose A. Scouler who conducts the clinic in Brownsville. Dr. Scouler testified that he began work in the tuberculosis clinic without pay in 1907, that he afterward received $300 a year and $600 per year and that since January, 1912, he has received $1,200 a year (p. 4639).

There is a civil service classification of "hospital physicians with maintenance, $1,800." Dr. Scouler testified that he was not attached to any hospital, that he conducted a clinic, and that he received $1,200 a year *without* maintenance (p. 4641). There is a position "attending physician *without* maintenance at tuberculosis clinic at $600 per year," but the four physicians mentioned received $1,200 a year each. The attention of Commissioner Keogh and Secretary Belcher was called to this condition, and neither of them could properly explain it. Dr. Scouler testified that he spent from 11 to 12 o'clock in the morning and from 2 to 4.30 in the afternoon at his clinic, and the other physicians when asked if their situation was the same with regard to compensation and service as that of Dr. Scouler, acknowledged that it was and their testimony under oath was not requested.

Pension Experts

A Clerk and an Accountant Appointed as "Pension Experts" and Permitted to Violate Civil Service Rules in the Office of the Municipal Commission Itself — An Actuarial Clerk and a Stenographer Also Excepted as "Experts" and Ordinance Against Non-Residents Evaded.

In the appointment of Robert Von Reutlinger and George B. Buck as "Pension Experts" the municipal commission abused the provisions of rule 12, part 6. Neither of these appointees was qualified in the degree required by law. Mr. Buck was slightly over 23 years of age when appointed on March 17, 1914, and one year and three months prior to that time, he was receiving at the rate of $1,200 a year as "clerk" in the employ of the efficiency commission in Washington, of which Dr. Frederick A. Cleveland, director of the bureau of municipal research, was chairman. Mr. Von Reutlinger was also employed by that commission, according to the payroll roster for December, 1912, as accountant at $1,800 per year. Mr. Buck testified (p. 4191) that he worked as actuary for the bureau of municipal research up to November, 1913, at $1,800 per year, that work terminating four months prior to his employment by the City of New York under rule 12, paragraph 6, as a "pension expert." The appointment of both Von Reutlinger and Buck was brought about by Henry Bruere.

Mr. Von Reutlinger was appointed on the same day as Mr. Buck and he was made chief of staff of the pension commission which he testified has 80 employees. He has been in the United States eight years, a citizen three years, and though recorded as an accountant with the efficiency commission in Washington, he acknowledged that his knowledge of bookkeeping was acquired while working as bookkeeper and clerk for a newspaper in Los Angeles (p. 4301) prior to his appointment with the tariff board in Washington in 1911. Secretary of the Treasury William McAdoo, in 1913, referred to Mr. Von Reutlinger as "inspector" for the tariff board when he requested the federal civil service commission to permit the establishment of an "efficiency commission" in the custom house, New York city, in the summer of 1913, at the request of John Purroy Mitchel, who was then customs collector.

With reference to Mr. Von Reutlinger's employment as "pension expert" by New York City, he testified as follows (p. 4302):

> "Q. You were never classified as an expert on pensions prior to your coming to New York City? A. *Never; as far as I know, there are no experts on pensions anyway.*
>
> "Q. What were you classified as when you were on the efficiency commission in the custom house (summer 1913)? A. I do not remember exactly; efficiency expert; that was it, I believe."

In the conduct of the office of the pension commission Mr. Von Reutlinger has flagrantly violated civil service law with the consent of the municipal commission. In the case of Alexander Grant, the violation was particularly reprehensible.

Grant was appointed as temporary clerk on August 6, 1914, though he is recorded on the civil service roster as "Hollerith machine operator" for temporary service under 12–4. On September 16 (ten days beyond the limit of provisional service), he was nominated for noncompetitive examination as "Hollerith machine operator" and qualified for examination as such on October 2. He acknowledged in his testimony that he knew nothing about operating a Hollerith machine (p. 4506), and that he was assigned to clerical work, his compensation being the same as second grade clerk, $600 per year. He further testified (p. 4508):

> "Q. How long did you do clerical work before you were finally put on experimental work on the machine? A. I should say it was about two weeks.
>
> "Q. Then you practiced on the Hollerith machine? A. Yes, I practiced at that, yes, sir.
>
> "Q. And you learned to work it? A. Yes, sir.
>
> "Q. And you have done some work on the machine since? A. Yes, sir."

In the face of Mr. Grant's testimony it is clear that the municipal commission permitted his appointment as "Hollerith machine operator" when he knew nothing whatever about the operation of such machine, and that he first learned it after his employment and while acting as clerk. An explanation of this condition is obtained from Mr. Grant as follows (p. 4509):

> "Q. How did you get your appointment to your present position? A. From Mr. Von Reutlinger.
>
> "Q. Did you know him? A. No, sir.
>
> "Q. How did you get introduced to him? A. My wife met his wife, and his wife introduced me to him and he *got me the position.*"

Mr. Grant testified that his wife was working as clerk in the office of the pension commission until the day before he testified (December 16), her employment having lasted thirty days. She was not selected from an eligible list. In explaining the appointment of Grant, Mr. Von Reutlinger testified (p. 3944):

> "Q. Was he taken from the civil service list? A. No, the civil service list was exhausted for *tabulators,* and we tried to do the best we can with outsiders.
>
> "Q. The civil service list of tabulators was exhausted? A. Yes, sir.
>
> "Q. And yet he is not doing tabulating work, is he exactly? A. *Not at the present time,* but he will do so probably tomorrow, and he has done it probably two or three days ago."

Mr. Grant in his application for noncompetitive examination for tabulating machine operator, states that he was employed as "temporary clerk" in the office of the Pension Commission. Yet the municipal civil service commission permitted him to continue as "clerk," though he was appointed as "Hollerith machine operator," and permitted him to be nominated for noncompetitive examination, though his only knowledge of that machine was what he acquired in the office of the Pension Commission after appointment.

The municipal commission also permitted the violation of civil service rules in its own office, in connection with the work of the Pension Commission. The State Commission on December 10th summoned Ernest Smith in charge of a clerical force in room 1438 of the municipal commission. He testified that he was supervising the work of this clerical force, filling in pension cards with data obtained from roster cards in the possession of the municipal commission, and that he had been so engaged since the middle of August (p. 3814). The record of the municipal commission shows that Mr. Smith was transferred as "structural steel draughtsman" from the bridge department to the Pension Commission on August 18, 1914, and no change of title thereafter is recorded, though the secretary of the municipal commission says that the title was changed subsequent to Mr. Smith's transfer to that of "draughtsman." His work was purely clerical. Similar work, that of transferring data from cards in various city departments to cards used by the Pension Commission, was done under the direction of Abraham Lazinsk, also a "structural steel draughtsman" transferred from the bridge department, and by Charles Baumgarten, also "structural steel draughtsman" who testified (p. 3884) that he instructs girls to fill out pension cards from data taken from other cards. He also operates a tabulating machine (p. 3885) and says his title has been changed to "draughtsman."

Another abuse of the merit system in the Pension Commission was the appointment of Leonard Stott Blakey as "statistician with special knowledge of economics" under rule 12, paragraph 6. Dr. Blakey secured employment as a *volunteer* with the commission during the summer of 1914, and engaged in correspondence with the officials of various cities with reference to pension matters, the purpose being to gather information on the subject (Von Reutlinger, p. 3932) "Q. Did Dr. Blakey see you or Mr. Bruere when he came here first? A. He saw Mr. Bruere and myself. Mr. Bruere referred him to me. Q. What did Mr. Bruere tell you about him? A. He just said — that is, what Mr. Bruere told me? Q. What did he tell you about him? A. He said, 'Dr. Blakey is going to see you, and if there is any work *that he can do there that is of interest to him and the commission, tell him to do it.*'"

Mr. Von Reutlinger testified that he recommended that Dr. Blakey be put on salary of $2,000 per year after two months of volunteer service (p. 3927) the municipal commission accepting him as an "expert." The ordinance relative to the employment of nonresidents was ignored by the commission which could only have sanctioned Blakey's employment under 12-6 as an "expert." Mr. Von Reutlinger's testimony indicates clearly that Dr. Blakey was not only *not* an expert, but that all he learned about the work required was during his service as volunteer during his college vacation. No "evidence in writing" could have been furnished the municipal commission that no one could be found in New York City competent to do the work, so Dr. Blakey was appointed as an "expert" to evade the ordinance.

In the case of Ralph Van Name, the municipal commission permitted the employment by the Pension Commission of a stenographer and typewriter at the rate of $1,800 a year *without examination* in the face of an eligible list for stenographers, without attempting to find out if any of those on the list were capable of doing tabulating work on typewriting machines. In order to permit this breach of Civil Service Law and rules, the municipal commission classified Van Name as an "expert" and covered his employment under 12-6. Van Name was not eligible for designation under 12-6 which permits the employment only of persons "engaged in private business." Van Name was employed by the city of New York as stenographer and typewriter for four years prior to his designation under 12-6 and was not engaged in "private business." He was stenographer in the office of President of the Board of Aldermen who suggested that he seek a transfer to the Pension Commission. Mr. Van Name was not in the competitive class then and could not be transferred. His engagement under 12-6 beginning April 1, 1914, was unwarranted and the testimony shows that Van Name did no other work than was done by other stenographers and typewriters in the office of the Pension Commission, except that he was in charge of that branch of service. His employment under 12-6 which was concurred in by the State Commission on the statement of the municipal commission, was an imposition on the state body, a breach of principle of civil service and an injustice to stenographers and typewriters on the eligible list.

In attempting to justify his appointment the witness claimed that it required a knowledge of pension literature to properly lay out the work for other stenographers and tabulators (p. 3897) "Q. Where did you get your special knowledge of pension literature? A. Since coming with the commission. Q. Then you didn't have that knowledge when you got this appointment? A. I did not, no, except I worked in a life insurance company for three or four years." (P. 3894). "Q. There are other stenoggraphers and expert tabulators doing the same work you are doing? A. Not experts. Q. They are stenographers and tabulators? A. Yes, sir. "Q. Working on the typewriting machines the same as you do? A. *Yes, sir, similar machines.* Q. Are the others employed under the same conditions that you are? A. No, sir. Q. They are civil service employees? A. Yes, sir. Q. At what salary? A. The two that I mentioned received $900 per annum."

The appointment of George B. Buck as "pension expert" at $3,600 per year merits further discussion. He was employed in 1910 and 1911 "or the beginning of 1912" at $1,000 a year in the census bureau in Washington (p. 4184). Then he worked for the Efficiency and Economy Commission in Washington (1912) at $1,200 per year, as "clerk" (p. 4186); then on the police pension fund, New York City, for the Bureau of Municipal Research (1913) at $1,800 (p. 4191). Then a short partnership with Herbert D. Brown, actuary, in Washington; then to the Pension Commission, at $3,600 per year as "expert." Prior to his partnership with Mr. Brown, Mr. Buck worked as actuarial clerk for Mr. Brown and he testified (p. 4207). "Q. How long had you been in partnership with Mr. Brown? A. About six months I should say. Q. And you left him entirely to come to New York? A. Yes, sir. Q. You are making more in the City of New York than you made as partner of Mr. Brown? A. Yes, Mr. Brown and I are not on good terms so I have to verify my statements otherwise." Mr. Buck testified that he was not a member of the Actuarial Society of America, the recognized organization for actuaries, but that he joined an actuarial organization in New York city *two months* previous to the date of his testimony, Dec. 14, 1914, and seven months after he begun work as "pension expert" for the city. Mr. Buck was living in Washington, D. C., at the time of his employment by the Pension Commission, according to his testimony (p. 4069).

Mr. Buck's advent to this city brought Edith B. Mangum, also from Washington, as "actuarial expert" under rule 12, paragraph 6, on April 15, 1914. The Municipal Commission excepted her under the $750 limitation and subsequently on November 28 raised the limit of compensation to $1,500 per year. Miss Mangum testified that she came here at the request of Chamberlain Bruere through Mr. Buck; that she was *assured* her salary would be $1,500 per year; that she was receiving $900 a year in Washington and was offered $1,020 per year if she remained with her employer there; but she declined (pages 4032–3 and 4). Her employment under 12–6 is unwarranted.

Commissioner of Accounts

In connection with the work of the Pension Commission, James McGinley, Chief Examiner of Accounts in the Commissioner of Accounts' office, testified (p. 4314) that 17 of the employees of his office, clerks, accountants and examiners, were detailed for a period of two months (some of them longer) to assist in organizing the work of the commission in the spring of 1914. These men were assigned to various city departments to have cards prepared by the Pension Bureau, filled out by city employees. The information of these cards was subsequently transferred to other cards by clerks in the employ of the Pension Commission. The testimony of Von Reutlinger (p. 3926) shows that 120,000 cards were used by the Pension Commission for gathering preliminary information. Mr. McGinley testified (p. 4315) that the Commissioner of Accounts loaned the Pension Commission at the request of Chamberlain Bruere, the services of two $3,000 a year men, one or two $2,500 a year men, some $2,100 a year men and some other employees drawing $1,800 or under. Harry F. Shields, a civil service fourth grade accountant attached to the Commissioner of Accounts' office, testified that he worked from June to October, 1914, for the Pension Commission, that he was assigned to the Borough of Queens and that he had charge of a squad gathering data on cards. "Q. (p. 4267) Had them filled in by employees in Queens Borough? A. Yes, sir. Q. And then brought them back to whom? A. To Mr. Von Reutlinger in charge of the Pension Bureau. Q. How many entirely, of the Commissioner of Accounts' office that you knew of, who worked with you for the Pension Commission? A. I think there were sixteen, if I am not mistaken. Q. Some of them accountants? A. Some of them, yes, sir. Q. Some of them examiners? A. Yes, sir. Q. Some of them clerks? A. Some clerks.

City Plan Experts

"Experts" appointed on Committee on City Plan, who Duplicate the Work of Other City Departments and Bureaus —Ordinance Prohibiting Employment of Non-Residents Ignored by Municipal Commission.

With the employment of George B. Ford as "expert consultant" to the Committee on City Plan of the Board of Estimate, began a series of exceptions from competitive examination which led to an appropriation of $30,000 for the work of the committee during the current year. The testimony of Mr. Ford and R. H. Whitten, secretary of the committee, discloses *a duplication of work done by other branches of the city government.* Mr. Whitten was exempted under Rule 12, paragraph 5, as a person "of high and recognized attainments," and Mr. Ford was appointed as an "expert" under Rule 12, paragraph 6, each at $5,000 a year, Mr. Ford's appointment beginning May 17 and Mr. Whitten's July 1, 1914. Mr. Ford testified that he made reports to the Committee on City Plan, of which President McAneny of the Board of Aldermen is chairman, among them being a report on the widening of Jackson Avenue, Queens Borough, to 100 feet. "Q. (p. 5747) What did you recommend? A. I don't believe I am called upon to say that. Q. That is a public matter, Mr. Ford; there is no secret about planning city streets. Q. (p. 5748) How did your recommendation differ from the recommendation of the engineer in the Highways Dept. in Queens, the Topographical Bureau of Queens? A. *I think it was confirma-*

tory. Q. Confirmatory? A. Yes, sir. Q. Then your work was duplicating their work, wasn't it? A. It was confirming it from another angle, from a general and different standpoint. Q. Who was the engineer of the Board of Estimate who went with you? A. Mr. Deutsch was there. * * * Q. (p. 5749) Did Mr. Lewis (chief engineer of the Board of Estimate) make a report on Jackson Avenue Boulevard in Queens? A. He did. Q. The Board of Estimate requested him to make such report, didn't it? A. Yes. Q. Do you know what recommendation was his? A. It is the same. Q. That has been the function of the chief engineer of the board of estimate many years. A. Yes, sir."

Mr. Ford testified that most of his reports to the committee on city plan are verbal. "Q. (5735) No record kept of what you report to them at all, just tell it to them orally and they act upon it; is that the way it is done? A. I should say that is the way the majority of it is done."

Mr. Ford testified that he was sent to investigate the request of the Botanical Society for an additional 150 acres in the Bronx. He declined to say what he reported on the ground that his report was "confidential" to the committee. "Q. (p. 5739) What report did you make on the Ft. George property? A. That was on the question of whether — of the extension of the city park area in the neighborhood of Ft. George. Q. Was your report in favor or against it? A. That is not a matter of public record yet; it is in committee.

* * * * * * * * * * * * * * *

Q. (5741) How long ago did you make your Ft. George report to the committee on city plan? A. I have not brought it up to the whole committee yet, only to the chairman of the committee; it has not been discussed by the whole committee. Q. (5742) Just by the chairman of the city plan committee? A. Yes, sir. Q. Mr. McAneny? A. Yes, sir. Q. Were you directed by Mr. McAneny to make a report with regard to the botanical gardens? A. Yes, sir. Q. Any other member of the commission direct you to make such a report? A. No."

Mr. Ford testified that he was working on a comprehensive plan for all matters which have to do with the physical development of the city and that by direction of Mr. McAneny he was

" working on schemes for the laying out of the district around the court house " (p. 5759).

" Q. (p 5752) Do you understand that your plan was to be adopted by the board of estimate? A. Not necessarily. Q. (p. 5753) What do you understand is to become of your plan for the court house site? A. Submit it to the various people who are interested in it, and they have a right to do as they want with it, they are not bound to accept it.

* * * * * * * * * * * * * * *

Q. The court house board did not ask you to do that work, did it? A. No. Q. No one but Mr. McAneny asked you to do that work, did they? A. No. Q. Do you make your reports; you must make your reports of your plan to Mr. McAneny? A. Yes, sir."

Mr. Ford testified that he had worked for the city planning commission in Newark and Jersey City (p. 5759); that he was not an engineer but an architect (p. 5763); that he had had nothing whatever to do with the laying of asphalt, wood-block or granite; that he never prepared specifications for any such pavements; but he acknowledged (p. 5761) that he recommended the laying of wood-block on Broad street, Newark, and that he had recommended various pavements for various streets in Jersey City, in conjunction with E. P. Goodrich, consulting engineer for the Borough of Manhattan.

Mr. Ford was questioned fully with reference to his knowledge of the ingredients in wood-block and asphalt, and he answered plainly that he was not familiar with them. All of which is cited to show that as " expert consultant " for the city-planning committee of New York City, Mr. Ford might make recommendations not based solely on his own judgment or experience.

Mr. Ford was employed as secretary of the heights of buildings commission during most of the year 1913, under a 12–6 appointment, at the rate of $3,000 a year. He is a member of a firm of architects which entered in competition with twenty-two others on plans for the new court house in Manhattan.

Besides Mr. Ford, the committee on city plan employs two other so-called " experts," each at the rate of $3,000 a year; both under the 12–6 rule. Though the compensation of one thus far is limited under the original appointment to $2,000 within the year, he is paid at the rate of $3,000. These "experts" have served continuously since their appointment, Mr. Ford on May 17, Herbert S. Swan on May 27, and the third, John P. Fox, on July 9, 1914. The provision of the rule under which they were appointed, provides only for "*occasional*" employment.

Herbert S. Swan was employed as "special investigator and expert statistician" by the heights of buildings commission, and his work terminated on December 31, 1913. He received compensation at the rate of $225 per month. Prior to that employment, which continued during most of the year 1913, he was in the service of the bureau of municipal research.

He testified that he was compiling the historical development of the street and park system in Manhattan Borough, which was part of a report that he was preparing for the committee on city plan. The data from which he is compiling his report was obtained from the records of *various city departments* and various public officials, and found in the public library or in the municipal reference library.

"Q. (p. 6231) And all your information can be obtained from the city departments or from the records of the city, city records somewhere? A. Yes, but that is only one of the features that — of the work that I have been doing. We have been doing work for the building district and restrictions commission."

Mr. Swan testified that he has resided in New York City five years (p. 6233), and that Mr. McAneny appointed him to the position of "expert investigator" for the committee on city plan. He was employed as "indexer" for the heights of buildings commission from February 26 to March 10, 1914, under rule 12, paragraph 4, preceding his engagement by the committee on city plan. His employment with the city plan committee was requested by President McAneny in a letter dated May 1, 1914, asking his exemption on the ground of "expert knowledge of city planning." This exemption was not allowed by the municipal civil service commission, which, however, permitted his engagement under the 12–6 rule. The municipal commission differentiates the 12–5 appointment as permanent and 12–6 as temporary, but the practical result of most appointments under 12–6 is the same as under 12–5 — permanent employment.

In the case of Sylvester Schattschneider, the rules were strained to permit his employment. Mr. Schattschneider testified (p. 3846) that he was employed in Harvard University to do "research work in sanitary engineering and vital statistics," prior to his employment by the committee on city plan on July 28, 1914, as "demographer;" (p. 3846) that he was engaged on "vital statistics" for the committee on city plan (p. 3848); and that he could not reconcile the work he was doing with the dictionary definition of the word "demographer," the title under which he was excepted by the municipal civil service commission and which means one who analyzes "vital and social statistics in their application to ethnology and anthropology." "Q. (p. 3849) How does that apply to your work, Mr. Schattschneider? A. That has no application to the work I am doing here. Q. Then you are *not* a demographer referring to the definition in the Standard dictionary. A. Not according to that definition. Q. But you are a vital statistician? A. *Yes.*"

Mr. Schattschneider testified that he procured his appointment with the city plan committee (3849) through Prof. Geo. C. Whittle, a member of the commission on building districts and restrictions; that he was engaged by Mr. Whitten, secretary to the committee on city plan (p. 3850); that Mr. Whitten told him he wanted a man to make a study of the population of New York City (3851).

"Q. (3852) And he went to Massachusetts to get him. A. Yes, sir. Q. You were a resident of Massachusetts and had not been in New York but how long? A. *I never resided in New York.*"

Mr. Schattschneider testified that since he entered upon his employment he has been engaged on a map of the City of New York indicating the census by putting "spots — black dots" on the map, each spot indicating twenty-five persons (p. 3844). He also uses other dots to indicate less than twenty-five persons each. "Q. (3843) Then you are going to have as many spots as twenty-five goes into the population, is that right? A. No, sir, in the outlying districts I have established a different or a smaller ratio of 10 or 5, because in the outlying districts the ratio of five would show us better."

Mr. Schattschneider testified that he was employed at the rate of $125 per month ($1,500 per year) (p. 3848), and that " the work I am doing now requires only a knowledge of a vital statistician."

Mr. Schattschneider was appointed under the 12–6 rule as " expert demographer " and the limit of his compensation had not been raised from $750 at the time he testified. In order that Mr. Schattschneider might be added to the city payroll, it was necessary for some one in authority to furnish " evidence in writing " that *no one could be found in the City of New York to perform the services required,* and the consent of the mayor had to be obtained to his appointment. In a letter to Mayor Mitchel, dated July 24, 1914, R. H. Whitten, secretary to the committee on city plan, makes this assertion: " It is impossible for the committee to secure a resident of New York City *having the peculiar and exceptional qualifications possessed by Mr. Schattschneider for the particular work required* " (p. 3862).

Secretary Belcher was asked if any effort was made by the municipal commission to ascertain if the statement made by Mr. Whitten was the truth, and he replied (p. 3867): " I do not know that any effort was made, any investigation."

Mr. Schattschneider could not have been employed by the city under the 12–4 rule, providing for emergency appointment for a temporary period, because of a city ordinance prohibiting the employment of persons who are nonresidents and noncitizens of the State of New York. His employment could only have been secured under rule 12, paragraph 6, classifying him as an " expert " for temporary service, and this was done by the municipal commission, which accepted the statement of Secretary Whitten that no resident of New York City could be found to do the work satisfactorily. Mr. Whitten's assertion, " having the peculiar and exceptional qualifications possessed by Mr. Schattschneider," is not a compliance with ordinance barring nonresidents from employment. The ordinance reads, " evidence in writing must be furnished that the services or work to be performed cannot be well done by any citizen and actual resident of the State of New York who can be discovered." No such evidence was furnished the municipal commission, judging from the testimony of Mr. Belcher (p. 3867).

By President Neu: "The only thing that you had was the letter of Mr. Whitten saying that such a person was needed?"

Mr. Belcher: "And Mr. Schattschneider's qualifications."

Mr. John P. Fox was appointed "expert and consulting engineer at $2,000" under rule 12, paragraph 6, according to the roster card of the municipal commission on July 9, 1914. He testified that he was being paid at the rate of $250 per month. The card shows that he was first employed by the city on May 28, 1908, as "expert statistician" for the metropolitan sewerage commission at $100 a month under rule 12, paragraph 6; that this rate was increased to $1,500 per year on September 9, 1908; that he was again employed as "building and sanitary expert" for the board of estimate and apportionment on December 16, 1912, and that his rate of compensation was raised to $2,250 a year on July 2, 1913. Mr. Fox was asked:

"Q. (p. 5845) Are you an engineer? A. I am *not* a civil engineer; I have no civil engineering degree. Q. Where do you get the title of engineer? A. Why, that comes through experience. * * *. Q. Was it allotted to you by any institution or college, or did you assume it yourself? A. No, sir; it was *bestowed upon me.* Q. By whom? A. I think Professor Swain of Harvard was one of the first ones to call me that. * * * . Q. Do you hold yourself out as a consulting engineer? A. Yes, sir. Q. And do you charge and collect fees? A. Yes, sir. Q. *As a consulting engineer?* A. *Yes, sir.* Q. Notwithstanding the fact that you have no degree as such, as a civil engineer or otherwise? A. *Yes, sir.* I prefer the title of 'municipal expert,' but the other title of 'consulting engineer' is more commonly used, and so I use that. Q. (p. 5852) Who gave you the designation of 'engineer' with the city planning commission? A. The committee on city plan. Q. Did they inquire of you whether you were or were not a civil engineer before they appointed you? A. *No, sir.* Q. Did you tell them that you were a civil engineer? A. *No, sir.* * * *. Q. (p. 5853) This is the first time it has been officially used with reference to your work, isn't it, 'consulting engineer?' A. Why, as far as I remember, *yes.*"

Mr. Fox is a member of the city plan commission of the City Club and of the city planning committee of the Citizens' Union.

Robert H. Whitten, who was exempted as secretary of the committee on city plan, at $5,000 per annum, has been a resident of New York State seven years, part of which time he lived in Albany. On May 6, 1914, the municipal commission gave a hearing on the proposed amendment to the civil service classification to exempt the secretaries of various new committees of the board of estimate, including the committee on city plan. This proposed amendment was opposed by Samuel H. Ordway, representing the Civil Service Reform Association, and George T. Keyes, assistant secretary of the association. July 1 Mr. Keyes again appeared before the municipal commission and opposed the exemption of Mr. Whitten on the ground that it had *not* been demonstrated that competition for the position was impracticable. Mr. Keyes said: "I concede Mr. Whitten's qualifications and enter the same argument with this addition: that competition has not been demonstrated to be impracticable. That is the one position which I was convinced ought to be filled through an examination, if not all of them, and this was the first one which converted me to competition — the secretary to the committee on city plan — and I think that commission has received from the first assistant chief examiner a plan for an examination for the position of secretary to the committee on city plan, which communication has received some consideration from this commission — a non-assembled plan."

Mr. Whitten was exempted under rule 12, paragraph 5.

Efficiency Engineers

Civil Service Rules Suspended to Permit the Employment of "Efficiency Engineers" and to Continue Them in the City Service.

The mania for "efficiency" produced a flood of 12–6 appointments in the "efficiency" bureau of the commissioner of accounts' office. One of these appointees is Samuel Thomas Goodwin, who was originally appointed in August, 1913. His rate of compensation was raised on October 29, 1913, to $1,500 and again increased on February 11, 1914, to $2,400. Mr. Goodwin was attached to the "efficiency bureau" of the board of estimate, which was afterward transferred back to the office of commissioner of accounts.

"Q. (p. 4169) You have been continuously employed Mr. Goodwin in the same bureau since August, 1913? A. Yes, sir, in the same bureau. Q. At what salary? A. From August until the latter part of — I guess until the end of 1913 at $2,700 and from then on at $2,400." Mr. Goodwin testified that he was engaged to make studies of the labor methods of the maintenance, highway and sewer bureaus of Richmond borough (p. 4171); that he made "suggestions" to one of the assistant engineers in Richmond with reference to "work programs" and that he "assisted in the design of a method for the control of work of the bureau of sewers and basin cleaning" (p. 4175). Witness testified that he was twenty-four years old and that his rate of pay was $8 per day during four or five months in 1912, when he worked for the commissioner of accounts (efficiency bureau) in the borough of Queens. Mr. Goodwin was changed to an emergency appointee (12–4) on August 1, 1914, and on September 29, his appointment was changed to 12–3 pending a competitive examination. Mr. Goodwin continued twenty-nine days *beyond* the specified time of thirty days as emergency appointee and he was carried *beyond* the stated period of two months pending competitive examination, the secretary of the municipal commission testifying that the examination would be held in "about a week" from the date the witness gave testimony, December 11 (p. 4163).

Albert J. Frohock, a resident of Philadelphia was engaged at $25 per day as "an expert with special knowledge of office procedure" on May 4, 1914. The limit of compensation under his original appointment was raised from $750 to $1,500 on May 28th, to $2,250 on July 22d, to $3,000 on September 2 and to $3,500 on November 18, 1914. Mr. Frohock testified that for one week subsequent to his employment, he commuted from Philadelphia to this city; that he afterwards boarded in East Orange, and then moved to New York City (pp. 4247–8). Mr. Frohock testified that he was engaged to investigate the mayor's departments (p. 4230); that he recommended changes in payroll and stenographic methods (p. 4230–1) and in office management in the tenement-house department (p. 4236); and that he was assisted in gathering material on which to base reports by an employee of the office of commissioner of accounts (p. 4240). Mr. Frohock testified that he was recommended to the acting commissioner of accounts, whom he did *not* know, by a man named Black who lived in Camden, N. J.; that Black had been requested to do some "efficiency work" for the city and that he (Black) brought Mr. Frohock to acting commissioner of accounts McGinley (p. 4248). "Q. Did you understand at the time of your original appointment that your compensation was not to exceed $750? A. No, I understood it will be possible an extension might be granted. Q. Was there an extension? Were you told it would be granted? A. They said they might possibly want me for *another month.*" *Four* extensions in compensation were granted Mr. Frohock by the municipal commission until the State Commission notified the local commission that no further extension would be approved. The final approval of the State Commission was obtained November 14, and Mr. Frohock was dropped from the service though he continued for seventeen days until December 2d (p. 4252). "Q. Were you relieved on December 27th? A. I had no — I understood when that extension was granted that the State Board would not grant any more, and that the time ended on the 2d of December. I received no notification from the office or from anybody else, until I asked Mr. McGinley about a week later."

Mr. McGinley testified (p. 4310) that he did *not* know Mr. Frohock prior to engaging him; that Mr. Black was suggested by Mr. Bruere or Mr. Lewis (deputy commissioner of corrections) and that he accepted Mr. Black's endorsement of Mr. Frohock as an "efficiency expert" though he did *not* know either (p. 4311). Mr. McGinley also testified that *several employees* of the office of commissioner of accounts worked with Mr. Frohock on his "efficiency" plans (pp. 4348–9).

Another "expert" who was engaged under 12–6 by the commissioner of accounts was Louis Ortner who was employed as "fuel expert and efficiency engineer" on February 6, 1914, at $10 per day. The limit of compensation was raised to $1,500 on April

8, to $2,250 on July 8 and to $3,000 on November 25, the final increase being concurred in by the mayor and the State Commission. Prior to his engagement as "expert" Ortner was employed in the department of water supply, gas and electricity as general inspector (exempt) at $3,000 per year, having been out of the city's employ a little more than a month before he was re-engaged as "expert." Mr. Ortner testified that he took *no* examination to enter the city service or to advance in it (p. 5191); that he passed from the water department to the commissioner of accounts and that he expected (December 28, 1914) to be transferred to the department of correction as "fuel expert and economical engineer" the first of the year. "Q. (p. 5196) Did Deputy Commissioner Lewis of the correction department tell you how much you would receive if you were appointed there? A. I believe he stated some estimate as between $2,500 and $3,000 — I believe." The State Civil Service Commission declined to approve any extension of Mr. Ortner's compensation beyond $3,000 and he had received no pay for "five or six weeks" (p. 5196).

An eligible list for economical engineers in the correction department containing twenty-four names was in existence at the time Mr. Ortner testified and the list is good until November 14, 1915. *The failure of the municipal commission to limit Mr. Ortner's services to the "temporary" period contemplated in the* 12–6 *provision, made it necessary for the State body to decline further extension in pay.*

John L. Mann was approved for emergency appointment as "Associate Efficiency Engineer" on July 22, 1914, at $2,700 per year and continued until September 29, *one month and twelve days beyond the* 30-*day limit* provided in rule 12, paragraph 4 under which he was appointed. He was then continued under rule 12, paragraph 3 pending competitive examination and again exceeded the time limit under this provision (two months) without having entered a competitive examination. His employment under 12–3 should not have extended beyond November 29, two months after non-competitive assignment. The competitive examination had *not* been held at the time Mr. Mann testified (December 11).

Mr. Mann testified that he was a friend of Mr. Welton, chief of the Efficiency Bureau of the Commissioner of Accounts' Office (p. 4154) and that he was assigned to work on Staten Island. "Q. (p. 4154) Had you ever been an 'associate efficiency engineer' anywhere else besides in the city service? A. I had nothing to do — *I had never had that title, no.* Q. (p. 4155) How long have you lived in the city of New York, Mr. Mann? A. Why, since — this last time since about the last of November, but I have more or less been here, I did not have a residence here. * * * Q. Where did you live prior to that time? A. Why, I lived in Santo Domingo in the West Indies."

Witness said he lived in Santo Domingo six years prior to coming to New York and was engaged in engineering work there (p. 4155), that he was "conducting a survey or physical audit to obtain work quantities, the physical and functional work qualities in the maintenance of highways in the Borough of Richmond" (p. 4156); also that he had been engaged on a scheme for "locational control of the work in the same borough" (p. 4158).

"Q. (p. 4159) You are trying to devise such a scheme? A similar scheme was laid down in the Borough of Queens by the Commissioner of Accounts — when was that, 1912, wasn't it? A. I think it was in 1912. * * * Q. (p. 4160) Was the scheme developed in Queens? Was it adopted there? A. I do not know, I think not, I think the scheme was rather complicated. Q. (p. 4160) You do not know whether your scheme of control will work out yet, do you? A. I have only been working on it a week and a half; I got just recently started on it. *It will take some months to try it out.*"

The witness is employed as "expert" on work which is *new* to him and of which he *had no knowledge whatever prior to his service with the city,* and the civil service rules *were violated in two particulars* by the municipal commission to continue his employment. There is no reason to believe that witness's ability as engineer is greater than that of hundreds of assistant engineers in the city service, *some of whom receive less than* $2,700 *a year salary.*

The case of Frederick R. Leach, shows a similar state of facts. Mr. Leach was appointed under 12–6 rule on November 1 last at $5,000 per year as " expert efficiency engineer " in the office of the Commissioner of Accounts. He testified that he was in charge of a squad of five other employees of the Commissioner of Accounts' office and that they were " installing a consolidated purchase system" in the twenty-eight departments of the city government controlled by Mayor Mitchel (p. 6020). He was working he said under an advisory committee of five members of whom Henry Bruere, City Chamberlain, is one. Mr. Leach testified that he was director of a Bureau of Municipal Research in Cleveland, five years prior to November 1 last; that he is working in conjunction with the Supply Division of the Bureau of Standards which is " standardizing " specifications for all city supplies. " Q. (p. 6029) How does it happen that you got that title (' expert efficiency engineer ') ? A. I don't know how it was, they just asked me to take up the work and I didn't pay much attention to the— "

At this point Commissioner Wolff of the State Commission called attention to the fact that Mr. Bruere had requested that the position occupied by Mr. Leach be exempted for that incumbent. " I told him I did not see how we could take a competitive place and put it into the exempt class," he added. Mr. Leach testified he did not know how long his work would last, but indicated that it could *not* be completed in a year (p. 6024). He is engaged under a provision for *temporary* employment.

The records of the municipal civil service commission show that James J. Pierson was employed by them on November 16, 1912, as " expert examiner " at $10 per day (exempt) ; that he was re-employed as " emergency civil service examiner " on February 1, 1913, under rule 12, paragraph 4, and on May 1, 1914, as " expert investigator " by the Commissioner of Accounts at $2,250 per year, under rule 12, paragraph 6. Mr. Pierson's testimony shows that he was entirely *unfamiliar* with the work to which he was assigned by the Commissioner of Accounts and at which he was engaged when summoned to testify on January 12, 1915. He testified that he was devising " score cards " for record of the work done by tenement house inspectors; that he had advised the consolidation of work done by food and milk inspectors in the Health department and that for the Charities department he reported on the "adaptability of the power house and coal bunkers" (p. 6421).

He also testified that before he began work for the Municipal Civil Service Commission, he was consulting engineer for the General Motors Company in Lansing, Michigan. He acknowledged (p. 6425) that he knew nothing whatever about the work to which he was assigned as follows: "Q. Do you know anything about what you have just described with reference to the taxicab inspectors prior to your being engaged by the city of New York? A. Oh, no, prior to being engaged. Oh no. My attention had not been drawn to it. Q. Did you know anything about the work done by the tenement house inspectors of the city of New York, prior to your being engaged by the city of New York? A. *The tenement house inspectors — no.*"

Department of Water Supply, Gas and Electricity

Civil Service Employees Dropped for "Economy" and Another Employed at Large Salary, Without Competitive Examination — Stationary Engineers Acting as Supervisors in Spite of Eligible List.

Under the administrations of Engineers Brush and Laase, employees are doing work inconsistent with their civil service titles. (pp. 5946, 6014, 6020, 6234, 6096, 6103, 6298, 6110 — Brower, January 21.) These violations include Thomas J. Norris, chairman, who has charge of the changes in the field, appointments, rejections, transfers; the preparation of budget estimates as to supplies and materials, statistical data, investigations of materials, etc.; Wilbur V. Gould, inspector of pipe laying, but is supervising the methods of ordering supplies and equipment; Carl A. Nolte, inspector of pipe laying, whose time is devoted almost entirely to litigation work, examinations of records, preparations for trials, attending on trials, etc. — in which work he really performs expert service far in advance of his civil service title and compensation; Harry S. Wooden, a topographical draftsman, most of whose work is clerical.

The testimony of Mr. Brower showed that there are three laborers in one of the Long Island divisions acting as stenographers and clerks. We were not able to go deeper into this situation but learned that the payrolls go on as in other departments with improper certifications. Two employees, Mr. Claussen and Mr. Brower, recently were forced out of places on Long Island, evidently because of personal feeling of the engineer, but ostensibly for lack of work. The work is now done by the engineer in charge of the division with the assistance of a clerk, through telephone and occasional visits, but the work must continue, and will have to be provided for in a short time by filling the places from which these men were dismissed.

Assistant Engineer Elmer G. Manahan was examined (p. 5985). He testified that in August, 1911, he was appointed assistant engineer in charge of the filter work at Jerome Park. He had no idea how he got the place; did *not* take civil service examination; he simply received a letter directing him to report to the chief engineer, and he found his salary fixed at $5,000. That filter work was discontinued and Mr. Manahan was out of a job, but one came as mysteriously as before, without request, and without knowing how it was done, he found himself transferred to take charge of the division of designing, in the department, at $4,500, with no examination. The division was in charge of Assistant Engineer Joseph Goodman, (salary, $3,250), who was doing well. He went in over Goodman's head and *the two are now doing the work that one did before.* Quoting:

" Q. Can you explain, Mr. Manahan, how it all happened? A. I think the explanation for that would have to come from my superiors. Q. You have just taken the good things Providence has sent you? A. That is all I have done. *I have never made application to be retained or to have anything done for me since I was appointed.*" He said the bureau of municipal research had been there — he had seen them.

Charles J. Clark (p. 5995), an assistant engineer, was on the filter works with Mr. Manahan. When the filter was discontinued, he was transferred with Mr. Manahan to the division of designing — with the same salary, $2,400. He displaced no one and was *added* to the force (which was getting along all right before he arrived).

William Drew and Harold H. Havill, stationary engineers in the water department, testified that they perform the services of supervising engineers, though a list for that position containing the names of several employees of the water department is in existence. Mr. Drew testified (p. 6100) that he has been doing supervisory engineers' work more than a year, and that he entered a promotion examination on December 28th (he testified on January 9, 1915), and that about twenty engineers entered the examination.

Mr. Havill testified that he took the same promotion examination and that he had been "advised" by Mr. Hancock, the supervising engineer, that it would be a good thing for him to do, to protect himself (p. 6109). Secretary Belcher of the municipal commission was asked if a complaint had been made during the preceding summer with reference to Messrs. Drew and Havill serving in a supervisory capacity in preference to those who were eligible for promotion, and he replied that such a complaint had been received and that in the case of Mr. Havill, a promotion examination was ordered to correct the assignment (p. 6100). "In the case of Mr. Drew, we were informed that the assignment had been corrected and that is under re-investigation. I do not think the report has been made yet."

The complaint to the municipal commission was made in the summer of 1914, and it was not until December 28th that the promotion examination to correct the wrong complained of was held. Those on the eligible list for supervising engineer will not be advanced unless it is as a result of the promotion examination. Mr. Drew testified that his salary as "assistant supervising engineer" was $2,500 a year, while the salary of other stationary engineers in the department is $1,750 or $1,800 per year." (See also pp. 6249, 6300.)

Committee on Taxation

Five "Experts" Excepted from Competitive Examination in One Small Committee of the Board of Estimate.

Another commission created by the Board of Estimate during the year 1914, which resulted in further abuse of the merit system, is the Committee on Taxation, of which Laurence Tanzer is secretary. Mr. Tanzer was appointed under 12–6 as an expert on "investigation of public questions" on June 26th, and he appointed a stenographer and a clerk. The Committee on Taxation which includes several prominent advocates of the single tax program, appointed Dr. Robert Murray Haig as "expert," to visit various cities in the United States and Canada, "to make an investigation of the system of adjusting or relieving improvements from taxation," and Mitchell P. Talmage "to investigate systems of special assessments in force in various cities." (P. 4517.) Dr. Haig has two assistants also engaged under the "expert" provision of Rule 12, one of them a student at Columbia University who is arranging his statistical data, and the other who is acting as stenographer (p. 4520); the former at $1.00 and the latter at 75 cents per hour. Mr. Talmage was still on his tour of investigation when Secretary Tanzer testified on December 16. His compensation agreed in advance, is $600 and expenses for three months, the compensation for Dr. Haig being $1,000 and expenses. Dr. Haig's tour was finished at the time Mr. Tanzer testified and he was preparing his report for the committee. The records of the municipal commission show that Mr. Talmage was employed by the Bureau of Municipal Research prior to his employment as "expert," and that he studied for six months in the office of the tax commissioner. Beyond that, his interest in taxation was confined to the management of his own property. Mr. Talmage is 28 years old.

Secretary Tanzer, whose salary is $4,000 per annum, was asked if he consulted the records of the municipal reference library for information on taxation in various cities. He testified (p. 4532): "There was a good deal of information there. Q. Covering many cities in the United States? A. Yes. Q. Canada? A. Yes. Q. Europe? A. Yes. Q. Australia? A. Yes. Q. Did you find information there covering the cities visited by Dr. Haig? A. Some of them. Q. Which cities that Dr. Haig visited did you find reports on or material with reference to the taxation in those cities, in the municipal reference library? * * * A. I am unable to state that. It may be that the municipal reference library contained information from *all* of those cities, but I am quite sure it contained none of the information which Dr. Haig was sent out to get."

A commission to develop new sources of city revenues sat for three years during the administration of the late Mayor Gaynor and rendered a report within two years including special assessments.

Standardization Experts

"Assistant Salary Standardization 'Experts'" Changed Into "Salary and Grade Examiners" and Maintained in "Emergency" Positions in Violation of Civil Service Rules.

The provisions of the Civil Service Law and rules were repeatedly violated by the municipal commission in order to enable the Bureau of Standards of the Board of Estimate to continue the services of so-called "experts" in "standardizing" salaries of city employes. In practically every case, the witness testified that he had no knowledge whatever of the work for which he was employed at $6, $8 or $10 per day, and several of them testified that they lived outside of New York city prior to their appointment. Practically all of them testified that they were appointed through influential friends and that they were unacquainted with the head of the Bureau, (then the Committee on Standardization of Salaries,) when they received their appointment under the Rule 12, Par. 6. This was during the year 1913 and their designation as "expert" under the 12–6 clause, *was renewed by the present municipal commission in* 1914.

In every case where such appointment was renewed, the municipal commission violated the provisions of Rule 12, paragraphs 3 and 4, in continuing these so-called "experts" in office as temporary and provisional appointees beyond the allotted period.

In two cases, the Municipal Commission continued the employment of provisional appointees who were barred from entering the competitive examination because they were over age.

The case of George W. Francis, is probably the most flagrant because Mr. Francis acknowledged on the witness stand that he had collected political campaign contributions from employes of the bureau, in the fall of 1913, and turned the full amount, $475, over to a superior in the office. Mr. Francis was still employed as "salary standardization expert" at $3,000 per year, at the time the investigation closed (January 22, 1915). He testified before the State Commission on December 9, 1914, as follows: (p. 3796.)

"Q. Did you not collect any contributions in the office—in the building during office hours? A. Did I collect any contributions?

By President Neu:

Q. You understand English, you don't have to ask the question again? A. I did not have to collect it, *the money was passed to me.*

Q. Who gave it to you? A. The man who volunteered the contributions. Q. Who were they?

Q. How much did Mr. Pemberton give you? A. I don't remember. * * * Q. How much did Mr. Newell give you? A. I don't remember.

Q. *How much did you contribute?* A. $20. Q. Did each of the others contribute the same amount? A. I don't think so. Q. Some more? A. Some less. Q. *Some* $15? A. *Yes, sir.* Q. *Some* $10? A. *Yes, sir.* Q. *How many contributed? How much did you receive entirely?* A. *The sum total of* $475. Q. *What did you do with the money?* A. *It was given to the campaign committee of the comptroller.* Q. Who was the campaign committee? A. Mr. Hervey was chairman, I believe. Q. *To whom did you give the money?* A. *Mr. Hervey.* Q. Do you know what Mr. Hervey did with it? A. No, sir. Q. The money was contributed by how many employes in the Standardization Bureau? A. *I won't say positively, I don't remember exactly but it was around* 20 *to* 22, *probably* 25. Q. Did any refuse to contribute? A. They volunteered the contribution. * * * Q. *Who made the collections?* A. *They came to me with the money.* Q. *Who gave you the money?* A. *They gave me the money.* Q. (p. 3806.) Did you give any receipts to any persons that contributed to the campaign? A. No, sir. * * * Q. *Did you know that it was a misdemeanor to make these collections?* A. If a man volunteers it? Q. *Did you know it was a misdemeanor to take it in your office? Did you know this is a violation of section* 26 *of the State Civil Service Law?* A. *I candidly admit, I did not.*"

Half a dozen "salary and grade examiners" testified that Francis sent them out in automobiles several days during the political campaign of 1913, to distribute slides of a candidate for re-election, to moving picture houses throughout the city, and one of them testified that he and others in the office addressed thousands of circular campaign letters to members of the Knights of Columbus organization by direction of Mr. Francis.

Mr. Francis was appointed an assistant salary standardization "expert" at $10 per day on February 1, 1913, under the 12–6 rule excepting him from competitive examination. He testified that prior to that time he had worked in Panama; that he was an inspector for the government and that his work in Panama ceased in January, 1913 (p. 3792). He said he had been in New York city only three weeks prior to his appointment in the city service.

Q. (p. 3792.) How did you get your position? A. As what? Q. The position you now hold? How did it originally come to you? A. Appointed by Mr. Tirrell and Mr. Hervey. Q. How did you get to him? A. Let us see — I don't know just how,— I was told by Mr. Sands of the Bureau of Municipal Research that there were certain positions that would be open, and that Mr. Hervey and Mr. Tirrell would be the men to appoint.

"Q. Mr. Sands sent you over to Mr. Hervey and Mr. Tirrell? A. He did not send me; he gave me his card to Mr. Hervey and to Mr. Tirrell. * * *. Q. Were you employed at once? How long before you were employed? A. No; it was probably two or three weeks."

Mr. Francis was continued as a 12-6 appointee until the end of 1913 and his services were renewed under the same provision as "expert" until April 29, when the position of salary and grade examiner was created by the board of aldermen. He was then appointed under rule 12, paragraph 4, providing for emergency appointment, which was continued under paragraph 3 of the same rule on June 29, pending the promulgation of an eligible list for the position. The municipal commission deliberately violated the provisions of both paragraphs 3 and 4 of rule 12 when they retained Francis more than one month as an emergency appointee and when they permitted him to remain longer than two months as a provisional pending the promulgation of the eligible list. Francis remained a provisional from June 29th to December 9th, the date he testified, a period of more than five months, and an emergency appointee from April 29th to June 29th, a period of two months.

In the case of William Van Wert, also salary and grade examiner in the same bureau, the municipal commission not only violated the provisions of rule 12, paragraphs 3 and 4 to permit him to continue in the service but they favored Van Wert with a second *noncompetitive* examination after he failed to pass the first, to make him eligible for the competitive examination. *Van Wert could not have been legally paid for the period of his provisional appointment under* 12–3 *had he not been passed in the noncompetitive examination.* Mr. Van Wert was employed at the rate of $6 per day on July 1, 1913. His employment was renewed under 12–6 as an "expert" by the present municipal commission until May 1, 1914, when he was changed into an emergency appointment under 12–4. He continued under 12–4 until July 2 (one month longer than the rule allows), when he became a provisional appointee under 12–3, and he was still carried as a provisional appointee when he testified on December 11th, exceeding the limit of time prescribed by more than three months.

Mr. Van Wert's mark in the first noncompetitive examination was 59 per cent, and then, by waiving rule 7, paragraph 12, the municipal commission ordered a re-examination. Examiner Fuld, who marked the papers in both examinations, testified he prepared both sets of questions and that he gave Van Wert the passing mark of 70 per cent. on the second examination. "Q. (p. 4330) On what ground was he re-examined? Why did the re-examination take place? Why was he re-examined, that is the question? A. I do not know; the commission decided that another examination should be given to him. * * * . Q. How often does it occur that those who fail in noncompetitive examinations are rerated? You say it happens frequently. How frequently? A. Well, it is pretty hard to say; I should say perhaps half a dozen times a year."

The first examination for Van Wert was on June 2, 1914. The second on June 26th. The provision of rule 7, paragraph 12, which was waived by the commission to enable Van Wert to take a second noncompetitive examination, provides that no person who fails in a noncompetitive examination shall be permitted to take a second examination *until after nine months,* provided that "for reasons to be set forth in its minutes this provision may be waived by the commission with relation to all such candidates in a given examination, *but not to any individual.*"

Secretary Belcher of the municipal commission contends that since Van Wert was the only candidate in the noncompetitive examination who failed that he was not barred by the rule from another examination to qualify for provisional appointment. If more than one person failed, Mr. Belcher contends, Van Wert could not have been given a second examination *alone.*

Mr. Fuld was asked (p. 4337): "Q. Do you consider that the questions asked in the first examination papers aided Mr. Van Wert in his answer to the second examination? A. It is rather difficult to answer that question because naturally the taking of one examination *would be of assistance to any one in taking a subsequent examination.* However, the questions were entirely different in the two examinations so far as they could be made different and yet maintain the proper parallelism."

The minutes of the municipal commission for June 17, 1914, contain a communication from the director of the bureau of standards requesting that Van Wert be given a second opportunity to qualify for temporary appointment under 12–3 on the ground that the questions asked in the noncompetitive examination on which he failed had to do with matters relating to departments *with which he had no experience as salary standardization "expert."* The letter from Secretary Belcher to the State Commission on December 8 bearing on this point explains that Mr. Van Wert had given practically all his attention to the department of public charities, and for that reason his knowledge was "specialized." The second examination included questions relating to the departments of charities and health, in both of which Mr. Van Wert had been employed.

Mr. Van Wert was asked (p. 4045): "Q. Had you learned anything from your first examination that was of value in answering the questions on your second examination? A. Why, somewhat; I knew the method under which the examinations were held and *some of the questions as to duties of other employees in other departments I had gone over and studied. Q. Some of the questions were almost alike, weren't they? A. Some of them were.* * * *. Q. (p. 4046) You were helped in answering the questions in your second examination by your experience in the first examination to some extent? A. A limited extent, yes."

Mr. Van Wert testified that "someone" recommended him for the position and that he took a letter of introduction from this "party" to Mr. Tirrell and Mr. Hervey, who appointed him. He was put to work drawing "functional charts" of various city departments under direction of Mr. Francis (p. 4054), and in his experience paper on the noncompetitive examination he mentions the fact that he had had one year's experience drawing "rough detail service charts of several departments" and "by continued assignment to these duties at Bellevue and allied hospitals and hospitals controlled by the department of health."

Fulton Colville, who lives in Atlanta, Ga., up to two and a half years prior to his being employed by this city as "assistant salary standardization expert" at $10 per day on January 7, 1913, testified that prior to his employment he was engaged in writing articles for magazines and newspapers (p. 4060). "Q. Had you any experience in appraising the value of employees in city, state or nation? A. No, not as such. Q. Had you any business with any department of the City of New York prior to your appointment? A. I had not. Q. (p. 4059) How did your appointment come about, Mr. Colville? A. *Why, I wanted a position and asked some of my friends who were connected with the city, who knew the place and one of them suggested this.* They called up Mr. Tirrell over the telephone and introduced me and I went over and had a chat with him and he asked me my qualifications and that I should write him a letter, and state what I had been doing and give reference."

Mr. Colville was continued as an "expert" under rule 12, paragraph 6, by the present municipal commission, until the position of "salary and grade examiner" was established on April 30, after which he was changed into a 12–4 emergency employee and then into a provisional appointee under 12–3, violating both provisions of rule 12, the same as was done in the case of Francis and Van Wert. He was put on a $2,400 salary basis when the new positions were created.

Edward H. Osborne was another "assistant salary standardization expert" turned into a "salary and grade examiner" when that position was created. Mr. Osborne testified that he was appointed on December 31, 1912, under rule 12, paragraph 6, at $8 per day and that his limit of compensation was raised and he was carried along under that provision until May 1, 1914, when his compensation was changed to $2,100 per year. Mr. Osborne was asked if he entered the competitive examination for the position of salary and grades examiner held shortly before he testified on December 9, he replied (p. 3770): "They would not let me. Q. Because you are too old. A. Yes. Q. You are still continued as a provisional employee? A. Yes."

Besides being carried longer than one month, from May 1 to June 29, 1914, under rule 12, paragraph 4, he was continued for more than five months under 12–3, his service under that provision being limited to two months. Rule 12, paragraph 4, provides for appointment to fill a vacancy in case of emergency and no "emergency" existed in the case of Mr. Osborne or the other "salary and grade examiners" who were appointed on April 30 or May 1 under 12–4. Mr. Osborne was asked what created the emergency (p. 3777) and he replied that he knew of no "emergency" because he had not been dropped from the service. "I have never been dismissed, that is all I can answer to that question."

There is no record that either Mr. Osborne or any of the other 12–4 appointees who were working under the 12–6 provision, were dropped from the service prior to their 12–4 appointment. It may be contended that the emergency was automatically created when the position of "salary and grade examiner" was established by the board of aldermen. The contention rests only on the supposition that the chief of the bureau of standards had it in mind to dismiss his 12–6 and 12–4 appointees and reappoint them at the same time. No such intention is visible in any of the records submitted at the examination. Mr. Osborne was asked (p. 3780) "Q. Never had anything to do with standardization of salaries or grades? A. No, sir. Q. Whatever you know or learned about that you learned after you went into this position, didn't you? A. Yes, sir.

* * * * * * * * * * * * * * *

Q. It didn't require any exceptional or especial scientific knowledge, did it? A. No, I don't think so. Q. Did you have any experience in city or state employment before you went there? A. No, sir."

Though Mr. Osborne, like Mr. Colville, was prohibited from entering the regular competitive examination for the position of "salary and grade examiner" because he was over 50 years of age, neither he nor Mr. Colville were prohibited from continuing in their position as provisional appointees and acquiring experience that qualified them for the work.

Fred T. Newell, another "salary and grade examiner" testified that he was in the insurance business prior to his appointment in February, 1913, that he lived out of town up to about a month before he was appointed "assistant salary standardization expert" at $8 per day; that he was raised to $10 per day in August, 1913, without examination (p. 3828) and that he continued on that basis until put on an annual salary the end of April, 1914, when the position of "salary and grade examiner" was established. His salary is $3,000 per annum. Mr. Newell testified that he had known Mr. Tirrell, director of the bureau of standards "ten or twelve years" (p. 3829), that he learned "they were going to make an investigation of some of the city departments" (p. 3830) and that he applied for a position. The provisions of paragraphs 3 and 4 of rule 12 were violated in his case, by the present municipal commission, the same as in the cases of other "salary and grade examiners" just cited.

Mr. Newell was asked (p. 3831) "Q. You never worked in any of the city departments or any of the state departments? A. No, sir. Q. Know nothing about the inside workings of the municipal or state offices? A. *No, not when I came in.* Q. Not until you got the job? A. No. Q. You learned it after that? A. Yes."

The commission examined eleven other "assistant salary standardization experts" appointed in December, 1912, or in 1913 at

$4, $6 and $8 per day. None of them knew anything about the work they were engaged to perform prior to their appointment as "experts" and practically all of them testified they were appointed through influential friends. (See testimony of Walter A. Johnson, p. 4093), Hoey and Jennessy (p. 3629), Peter B. Scanlon (p. 3644), Walter F. Clayton (p. 3662), Mortimer Green (p. 3680), Wm. L. Kavanagh (p. 3693), Julian B. Thomas (p. 3720), Frederick C. Schmidt (p. 3736), Wm. W. Colne (p. 3740), James C. Wilson (p. 3784), and Walter A. Johnson (p. 4093). Some of them were dismissed after the election in November, 1913, and the remainder in February, 1914. Two or three of them, according to Mr. Tirrell, director of the bureau of standards, were dismissed soon after their appointment on the ground that they were *not qualified.*

Board of Education

"Inspector of Masons' Material" Buys Pianos — "Inspectors of Masonry and Carpentry" Buy Furniture in Board of Education.

The building bureau of the board of education furnishes a grotesque violation of civil services in the case of Caleb Cameron "inspector of masons' material." Mr. Cameron is a relative by marriage of C. B. J. Snyder, superintendent of buildings, and has occupied a position in the bureau since 1895. He receives $2,860 per year, which is nearly $1,000 more than is paid to other "inspectors of masons' material," and *has never passed a civil service examination for his position.*

Mr. Cameron testified that he was not a mason by trade when appointed to the position (p. 3602), and that part of his time is occupied purchasing pianos and writing specifications for pianos for the new schoolhouses; also preparing the city's defense for the corporation counsel in suits brought by contractors on new school buildings (p. 3594). Mr. Cameron testified that he has purchased pianos for new schools for many years, and he acknowledged that he had never constructed a piano or organ though he prepares the specifications for these instruments. "Q. (p. 3598) How do you qualify to write specifications for pianos when you are an inspector of masons' material? A. Well, I am a musician. I have been an organist. * * *. Q. (p. 3602) What are your qualifications for inspector of masons' material? Did you pass an examination for the position? A. No. * * * Q. What is your trade? A. I had not any trade. Q. You are not a builder, a mason, a stone mason or anything of that kind? Never worked at any of those things before you became inspector? A. No, sir."

Mr. Cameron testified that he inspects the cement, limestone, enamel brick and bluestone received by the city for use in its school buildings, and that he occasionally goes out of town to inspect materials before they are sent to see that specifications are complied with.

Trimble Foster, an "inspector of masonry and carpentry," testified that he was in charge of the furniture division of the building bureau; that for seven years he has inspected furniture, not masonry or carpentry, and that he has other "inspectors of masonry and carpentry" inspecting furniture for him, such as desks, chairs, etc. Mr. Foster's roster card gives his designation as "building inspector," though he is entered on the payroll of the board of education as "inspector of masonry and carpentry." (See Payrolls, pp. 6552–3).

Several other "inspectors of masonry and carpentry testified before the commission that they were performing the duties of general inspectors on new school buildings," that they were responsible for all the work done by subcontractors on these buildings; that they inspect iron work, steel, plastering, all kinds of repairs, the installation of plumbing, electrical and steam heating plants and the construction of fireproof stairways. (See testimony of Samuel Lord (p. 3612); Daniel J. Gillespie (p. 3616), James R. Mulligan (p. 3621), James Quinn (p. 3624), Patrick F. Harney (p. 3626).

Payrolls were inspected by the State Civil Service Commission and it was found, as in other cases, that the officials of the department had made the usual *false* certificates that the inspectors had performed only the work appropriate to their civil service titles.

Law Department

Law Department Employees Favored by Questions in Examination for " Law Examiner."

On November 9, 1914, the municipal commission held an examination for " examiner law department," and complaints were received by the State Commission that two of the ten questions favored candidates in the office of the corporation counsel. The questions complained of are, " What is meant by ' vouching in ? ' " and " What is meant by ' an action over ? ' "

In explaining the reason for these questions, Examiner Elmer G. Story, in a letter to the chief examiner of the municipal commission, to whom the complaints were referred, wrote: " The expression ' vouching in ' is a familiar one in connection with the duties of the position, also it is one frequently used in law offices and claim departments having to do with negligence cases." He also says, with reference to the other question, " What is meant by ' an action over,' " as follows: " I think the expression is known to investigators outside as well as inside of the corporation counsel's office."

The State Commission wrote to the claim department of the Brooklyn Rapid Transit Railroad asking if the two expressions used in the examination were known to them and received the following response (p. 6313):

" Replying to your favor of the 21st instant, I beg to say that the terms ' vouching in ' and ' an action over ' *has never been used by this department."* Signed, I. Isaacson Gen'l Claim Ag't.

In view of this statement the municipal commission should revise the questions in the examination so that no advantage is given to candidates employed in the city's law department where the two expressions are commonly used.

Civil Service Rules Violated in City's Law Department

The provisions of the civil service rules are violated in many departments of the city government, including the municipal civil service commission itself; and there are violations even in the city's law department. Joel J. Squier, assistant corporation counsel in charge of the bureau of street opening, was summoned as a witness. He testified frankly and acknowledged that fully a dozen employees in his bureau were working outside of their civil service titles. He told of a clerk in his office who is generally engaged in preparing legal papers, and who examines the qualifications of condemnation commissioners before the Supreme Court; of a clerk who does computer's work though there is a civil service classification for both; and of computers who do clerical work (p. 3515); of two clerks who do stenographic work though there are lists for both clerks and stenographers in existence; and of other employees whose services are not according to their civil service designations.

Police and Fire Departments

Many assignments of uniformed policemen and firemen to duties other than those performed by the rank and file in the departments, were reported to the State Commission, which obtained from both departments lists of uniformed men so detailed. In most instances, the detail seemed unavoidable though in others the detail was improper. On the whole, this commission is satisfied that the wrong assignments will be or have been corrected.

"Occasional" Service For Long Periods

"Experts" Appointed for "Occasional" Service. Have Held Office Several Years By Consent of Municipal Commission.

A striking illustration of the abuse of the 12–6 rule is the case of W. Richmond Smith, chief of the Division of Supplies, Bureau of Standards of the Board of Estimate. Mr. Smith was appointed on May 1, 1910, as "expert statistician" at $3,600 per year and his 12–6 designation *renewed* each year including 1914, when his compensation was raised to $5,000. During the past two years he was designated on the roster cards of the municipal commission as "expert in charge," his function of "statistician" having descended to a successor at $3,000 per year.

Mr. Smith testified on December 21, last, that he was *not* a citizen of the United States (p. 4857); that he had been in this country since 1907 (p. 4859); that he secured employment on a New York newspaper and after two years was employed by the comptroller as "expert," in 1910. Mr. Smith testified that he was not originally appointed as "expert statistician," but as "expert in charge of the bureau of standards" (p. 4834) though he acknowledged that when first appointed he took the minutes of the meeting of the Commission of "experts" who were appointed to "standardize" specifications for supplies. Two of these "experts" had been appointed under the 12–6 rule, while the others on the commission were drawing pay from the city through various city departments, or were giving their services as "experts" gratis. One of these "experts" appointed under 12–6 was Col. Charles N. Swift, who appeared as a witness and testified (p. 4872):

"Q. What did the Committee do when it organized? A. Well, when the committee was first organized, it appointed a clerk, the chief clerk, Mr. Smith was brought in, and Mr. Fisher said: 'This will be our chief clerk. He has some knowledge as an expert.' Q. Did Mr. Fisher say what kind of an expert Mr. Smith was? A. No, he did not. Q. Did Mr. Smith take the minutes of the meeting? A. Yes, *he always took the minutes.*"

Mr. Smith's employment under 12–6 is a clear violation of the intent and purpose of the rule which contemplates only "occasional" services and not such as rendered continuously by Mr. Smith. Mr. Smith testified that following his employment as "expert" without civil service competition, he acquired considerable knowledge of the work required for the conduct of the supply division of the bureau of standards. "Q. (p. 4857) You learned a great deal about standardizing after you were appointed to the position, didn't you, Mr. Smith? A. *Naturally.*"

The municipal commission made no effort to correct the method of Mr. Smith's employment, continuing him throughout the year 1914 as a 12–6 appointee, after four years of service under the same classification. The fact that Mr. Smith acquired "expertness" in the service is no vindication of his appointment which contemplates only "occasional" and temporary service.

A further abuse of the merit system in the division of supplies, bureau of standards, is the case of John F. Donovan "expert statistician" at $3,000 per year. Mr. Donovan was appointed under 12–6 in 1911 at $1,800, and he has been carried under the exception clause ever since. Donovan's exception was renewed by the present municipal commission on January 1, 1914 and 1915.

The division of supplies also employs a "price expert" at the rate of $2,000 per year, his appointment under 12–6 having begun on November 12, 1912. It was renewed a year later and was continued through the year 1914 by the present municipal commission. It was not until November 16, 1914, after two years as a 12–6 appointee, that the municipal commission ordered an examination for the position held by Mr. Roure, the "price expert" (p. 4551); *this action being taken three months after the investigation of the municipal commission began.*

Prior to his employment as a "price expert" Mr. Roure was engaged following the ticker in a newspaper office and reporting the fluctuations of the stock market. He had no experience whatever in the purchase or sale of commodities or in the fluctuation of prices through service in any of the commercial exchanges. The title of "price expert" is a misfit and should be changed to more closely apply to the position.

The intent and purpose of rule 12, paragraph 6, was violated in the appointment of J. Raymond Kiefer as "expert examiner" on June 9, 1914, at the rate of $8 per day. Mr. Kiefer had been a 12–6 appointee as "special investigator" since August 18, 1913, employed by the bureau of standards, supply division. His appointment was a *renewal* of his previous engagement. The 12–6 rule provides for the employment of persons "in private life." Mr. Kiefer was an inspector in the bureau of highways, Manhattan, prior to his appointment in August, 1913, and previous to that was for four years inspector and engineer in the board of water supply. His rate of compensation was changed from $8 per day to $2,100 per year in September, 1914, when the grade of "examiner of purchase and supplies" was established, but no record of his emergency appointment under 12–4. No request for the extension of his compensation beyond the limit of $750 provided under 12–6 has been made to the municipal commission, and Kiefer swore (December 16) that he had drawn no pay since September when the limit of the $750 compensation was reached (p. 4661).

No competitive examination for the position of "examiner of purchase and supplies" has been called by the municipal commission and Kiefer and another person, Joseph Byrne, hold that position without civil service warrant. They are both 12–6 appointees and Kiefer testified (p. 4651) they have been doing the same work since and before their re-appointment in June, 1914.

"Experts" Who Drew Fancy Salaries from the City

A flood of light was shed on the subject of "experts" employed by the city by the testimony of F. C. Rippon, who was engaged as "expert accountant" for the committee on school inquiry, of which John Purroy Mitchel, then president of the board of aldermen, was chairman. Mr. Rippon's compensation was $8 per day and he continued under rule 12, paragraph 6, from December 23, 1912, to January 24, 1914, when he became secretary of the department of correction. Mr. Rippon testified that he was glad he did not have to serve as an "expert" any longer. He felt more comfortable as a plain secretary (p. 5454). Mr. Rippon testified that he received $2,400 per year with the Efficiency and Economy Commission in Washington in 1912, and that following that employment he came to this city, having been introduced by a Mr. Proctor, who worked with him in Washington. He said he lived in Philadelphia prior to going to Washington and that he lived in New York City *only from the time his employment began.* He secured his appointment as secretary to the correction department through Deputy Commissioner Lewis, and his salary was increased from $2,500 to $3,000 on January 1, 1915. As secretary he is a member of the promotion board in the department, though *not* a competitive civil service employee himself.

Mr. Rippon testified that he understood an "efficiency engineer" to be one who was able "to criticise and invent new methods" and that if he didn't find anything to criticise he would not have a job. He said "efficiency engineers" made many reports and wrote up many statistical cards, and that very often the data compiled by them is filed away and never used (p. 6453).

In this connection, the testimony of Edmund D. Fisher, deputy comptroller, and George L. Tirrell, director of the bureau of standards, is interesting. Both said they had little faith in the title of "expert" or "efficiency engineer;" that the title meant nothing to them with regard to the relative ability of individuals.

The school inquiry committee, which finished its work in December, 1913, employed many high-priced "experts," one of whom, Dr. Frank P. Bachman, employed through the influence of the bureau of municipal research, drew more than $7,000 up to the end of 1913, and he drew $1,560 from January 1 to June 24, 1914. He was carried as an "expert" under rule 12, paragraph 6, up to December 31, 1913, and on January 1, 1914, was continued under 12–3 as a provisional employee until his services ceased, more than six months later. The spirit of civil service law and the intent of the provision under which he was appointed were violated by the municipal commission, which continued him under 12–3 *four months longer than provided under the provision.* Efforts to locate Dr. Bachman were unavailing.

W. F. Clowes, another "expert" for the board of estimate, was carried under 12–6 at $8 per day as "manuscript editor" until July 9, 1914, having drawn $2,140, and Tristram W. Metcalfe and George W. Goeller have continued as "publicity experts" for the board of education for several years, the limit of their compensation being $750 a year.

Another "expert" was employed by the committee on school inquiry at $20 per day for nine months. Deputy Commissioner of Correction Lewis, who represented Mr. Mitchel on the committee, said the money paid to him was wasted, because his report was rejected.

Louis B. Blan, who conducted an educational news service, was engaged by the committee on school inquiry as "educational expert" at $15 per day on January 24, 1913. He was continued under that designation and the limit of his compensation raised from $750 to $3,970 within the year. Blan was re-employed as an "examiner of accounts" in the office of commissioner of accounts in April, 1914, and he has drawn at the rate of $3,000 per year since. The position of "examiner of accounts" is exempt, because the service performed by such employees is considered *confidential.* The testimony of Mr. Blan shows that he has virtually acted as publicity agent for the municipal administration since he became "examiner of accounts" (p. 5014).

Finance Department's Employees Working as "Exempt" in Spite of Fact that Exemptions Were Denied

The State Commission discovered that in the case of Paul Loeser, Joseph H. Eustace and Robert G. Newbegin the denial by the municipal commission of the request for their exemption under 12–5 was circumvented by their retention on the payroll of the comptroller's office though they were doing the service for which their exemption was requested. Mr. Loeser, who holds an exempt position as "expert accountant" in the finance department, testified on December 14th that since April, 1914, he has been employed in the bureau of standards of the board of estimate (p. 4258) as assistant to Director Tirrell. According to the minutes of the municipal commission, read in evidence (p. 4260), the board of estimate organization committee, of which the comptroller is a member, requested the exemption of Loeser and the two others mentioned. The request was denied on June 3d, two months *after* Loeser began work with the bureau of standards, and Eustace and Newbegin in the bureau of contract supervision of the board of estimate, under Director Adamson. Neither Loeser nor Eustace nor Newbegin have been restored to their former places in the finance department and were at work in their new positions at the time they were summoned to testify, Loeser on December 14 and Eustace and Newbegin on a subsequent date, in spite of the fact that their exemptions had not been granted.

Department of Parks, Borough of Brooklyn

How Peter Ward Brennan Became an Exempt Supervisor of Recreation.

By action of the Municipal Civil Service Commission, March 4, 1914, Peter Ward Brennan was excepted from examination under the provisions of clause 5 of Rule XII, for appointment as supervisor of recreation in the department of parks, Borough of Brooklyn, salary $1,200 per annum. The commissioner of parks, in that borough, requested that the position be exempted under the title supervisor of play-grounds, but the request was denied, without prejudice to the submission of an application for suspension of the rule requiring examination in the case of a particular individual. The refusal of the municipal commission to exempt the position was based, on the ground that the compensation was too low to make competition practicable. The municipal commission states that it was satisfied with Brennan's qualifications and, therefore, approved his appointment. Later in the year, when the State commission raised the question as to the propriety of this action, the municipal commission concluded, quoting from its annual report, that its action "*had not been strictly in keeping with the provisions of the rule and it, therefore, rescinded its action and ordered a competitive examination.*" The excuse for the error in the case of Mr. Brennan, is given in the language of the municipal commission as follows: "In the past, exceptions under rule XII, clause 5, have been allowed without full and detailed information as to the candidate's qualifications."

The investigation into the case of Brennan came about through the suspension of Herman Fels, who was gymnasium attendant, for alleged neglect of duty. It appears that he had an unfair trial. He was "undesirable" because he insisted that Mr. Brennan was not professionally qualified for the place to which he had been appointed, and that some of his statements with reference to previous employment, were not true. He and a Mr. Friedman considered that they had a right to compete for the position. Fels testified that Brennan, who made the alleged false charge against him, said that he would make an example of him because he was keeping a diary (of events in the department). This matter was pending before our commission and the witnesses were present at many hearings before they were called. The action of the local commission was not taken until after the witnesses, Fels and Friedman, had been seen in the hearing room and the local commission was fully aware that the matter was to be taken up by our commission.

Mr. Brennan was dropped from his position by order of the local commission, but he was still continued in the employ of the park department in Brooklyn when this investigation closed. (See pp. 2920, 2922, and 2942.)

How Henry Wilkens was Changed from "Food Inspector" to "Inspector of Repairs and Supplies" and to "Confidential Inspector."

An interesting witness before the commission was Henry Wilkens, employed as "confidential inspector" in the charities department. Mr. Wilkens testified that he was employed on January 19, 1914, as "food inspector" at $1,200 per year; that he continued under a 12–4 designation until April 17, when he became a 12–3 provisional appointee, and continued as such until September 6, when he resigned because an eligible list was promulgated. He was *not* on the list, not having entered the examination, and he was carried for *four and a half months* as a provisional appointee when the limit of time provided under the rule was *two* months. Mr. Wilkens testified that his non-competitive examination included twelve questions on food, but that he was *not* examined as to his feet, heart, lungs or body though the position of food inspector requires considerable walking. (p. 1215.) From September 6 to October 6 Mr. Wilkens was carried as an "inspector of repairs and supplies" at $1,650 per year, and that from October 6 to the time he testified, he was "confidential inspector" in the Charities Department at $1,350 per year. He acknowledged that though he has had three titles and salaries since his services began, his work *has never been changed.* Mr. Wilkens was asked how the change to confidential inspector was made and he replied (p. 1213) "I was merely notified by Mr. Borden that my services as 'inspector of repairs and supplies' terminated. I then asked him — I said 'I walked out then.' I was notified by Mr. Borden to wait a few days, and then I was appointed confidential inspector."

Examiner Instructed to Give Credit for Experience to "Temporary" Salary and Grade Examiners.

In connection with the examination for "Salary and Grade Examiner" recently held, the testimony of special examiner Thomas Garrett, Jr., shows that special advantage was given those who were appointed temporarily to the position with the consent of the municipal commission. Mr. Garrett testified on January 15 (p. 6499): "Q. Did you take into consideration and give credit for experience to those who were working on the Board of Estimate Committee as salary and grade examiners? A. Yes. Q. What was your instruction in reference to that? A. I was instructed by the Commission to give credit for the service in that position. * * * Q. Did you understand that those persons who were working as salary and grade examiners were temporary employees? A. Yes, sir. Q. Did you say in advance to your co-examiner, Mr. Storey, or to the Commission, that you did not think any credit should be granted for such experience? A. I knew the rules were such that under ordinary circumstances credit should *not* be given for experience in some positions of that sort, on account of the holding over under temporary appointment. Q. And when you began to mark the papers did you begin with instructions to give credit for such experience, and did you mark them without giving credit for such experience? A. I marked them *without* giving credit at all at the beginning. Q. And then what? A. And then I received instructions to *give* credit for such service. Q. From whom were those instructions? A. I have forgotten whether it was a letter from Mr. Murray or from Mr. Ireland, I have forgotten which. Q. From the Commission? A. From an officer of the Commission; it might have been Mr. Murray or Mr. Ireland; it might have been the secretary; I have forgotten which."

Civil Service Rules Evaded to Promote Engineer C. U. Powell

Civil Service rules were evaded and the evasion was concurred in by the municipal commission, when Charles U. Powell was appointed assistant engineer in the Borough of Queens at $3,000 per year on April 22, 1914, as a provisional appointee. Mr. Powell continued under that provision until August 27th, when he was favored with a promotion examination in which he himself was the only candidate, passing with a percentage of 85.83. After that date Mr. Powell became a permanent appointee as assistant engineer, Grade E, in charge of the Division of Substructure and Franchises in Queens Borough.

Mr. Powell *failed* to pass the promotion examination for assistant engineer, Grade E, held on June 10, 1913, at the request of the president of Queens Borough. Nine candidates entered that examination, of whom three passed, first on the list being Leon M. Schoonmaker. Mr. Powell's mark was 67 per cent. on technical knowledge, which disqualified him. In December, 1913, following this examination, the acting borough president of Queens requested the municipal commission to recognize the division of substructures and franchises, newly created, in promotion examinations.

On April 6, 1914, President Connolly of Queens Borough, requested that a promotion examination for assistant engineer, Grade E, in the Division of Substructure and Franchises, be called. The only person eligible was Mr. Powell, who, as stated, received a passing mark. His salary was then increased permanently from $2,250 to $3,000, at which rate he was paid since April 22d, when he was provisionally appointed to the higher grade.

The work performed by Mr. Powell as chief of the division of substructure and franchises was formerly performed by an assistant engineer in the topographical bureau, and the commission is informed that the position was again incorporated in that branch of the engineering service in Queens on January 1, 1915. It would seem as if the division was created rather for the purpose of advancing Mr. Powell than for facilitating or improving engineering service in Queens Borough. Mr. Powell was the only engineer employed in the division since it was created. Mr. Schoonmaker, who passed first on the promotion examination in June, 1913, was promoted to principal assistant to the engineer in charge of the topographical bureau.

Mr. Powell's provisional appointment from April 22 to August 27, 1914, exceeded the limit provided in paragraphs 3 and 4 of rule 12, under which he was appointed, by one month. There were other assistant engineers in Queens qualified for the promotion examination which Mr. Powell alone took, but the decision of the commission to recognize the new division as a separate entity in promotion examinations, debarred others from entering. (pp. 6314 and 5185.)

State Commission's Refusal To Exempt Positions Influenced Municipal Commission

President Moskowitz prides himself on the fact that the municipal commission denied the request of President McAneny of the board of aldermen, representing the members of the board of estimate, for the exemption of the positions of secretaries to the six newly created committees of the board of estimate: the committee on city plan, committee on social welfare, committee on port and terminal facilities, committee on education, committee on markets and committee on revision of city charter.

The request was *not* denied until after Samuel H. Ordway, chairman of the executive committee of the civil service reform association and George T. Keyes, assistant secretary of the association, appeared in opposition to the request at the meeting of the municipal commission on May 6, and not until *after* the State Commission declined to exempt from competitive examination, the position of assistant secretary to the mayor which had been created for two incumbents. This request to exempt the positions was submitted to the State Commission by the municipal commission early in the spring of 1914, and the State Commission replied that it saw nothing of a confidential nature in the work to be performed by these two assistant secretaries, particularly since the mayor now had two exempt secretaries. Mayor Gaynor had *no* assistant secretaries in his office.

In the case of the secretaryship of the committee on city plan, the appointee, Robert H. Whitten, was excepted under 12–5 by the municipal commission in spite of the protest of Mr. Keyes of the reform association and in spite of the report of the advisory board of the municipal commission composed of the assistant chief examiners, who drew up a plan for an examination. In explaining why this plan was not carried out, President Moskowitz said (p. 6479): "The commission — you see, when it considered the name of Whitten, they thought that he represented such a high type of person, such a high calibre, one of the leading men in the city planning of the country, and in view of the fact that this was a new departure, it wanted to experiment with some examinations, and it did, and in view of Mr. Whitten's very high qualifications he was passed under the 12–5." (See section on city plan committee.)

In the case of the committee of the board of education, Mrs. Mathilda Ford, who is a civil service employee, was appointed to the position which was classified, and Moses Altman, a civil service employee, became secretary of the committee on charter revision, which was also classified. That left only the committee on social welfare, committee on markets and committee on port and terminal facilities without secretaries. The request of Comptroller Prendergast and Dock Commissioner Smith to exempt Kerner Easton, secretary to the committee on port and terminal facilities, was granted by the municipal commission *in spite of Mr. Easton's confessed disqualification for the exemption* (see report on Kerner Easton's exemption elsewhere); and the appointment of Anthony P. Ludden as secretary to the committee on markets under 12–4, as an emergency appointee, was *unwarranted* in the face of the adverse reports made by the examiners and special examiners for the municipal commission (see report on Ludden elsewhere).

The municipal commission, according to Dr. Moskowitz, has advertised the examination for the position of secretary to the committee on social welfare, and this is the only new secretarial position in the board of estimate that has not yet been filled by the person originally selected by the board when it requested that all new secretarial positions be exempt. *The net result of the municipal commission's action in these cases is the same as if the positions were exempted;* the incumbents desired for them under such exemption now occupy the positions. In order to accomplish this result, the municipal commission *deliberately violated the intent and purpose of civil service rules when it permitted the appointment of Kerner Easton and Anthony P. Ludden to the secretaryships above mentioned.*

After the State Commission denied the request of the municipal body to exempt the two new positions of assistant secretary in the mayor's office, Mayor Mitchel appointed E. Stagg Whitin as a "temporary" assistant secretary on May 18. The municipal commission classified him under rule 12, paragraph 4, which permitted his appointment for thirty days. He was carried under that provision until June 16 and his services were not discontinued until October, exceeding the limit of the provision of paragraph 3, under which he was continued from June 16, by about two months. In order that the mayor might employ two new assistant secretaries, it was necessary to create those positions by action of the board of estimate and board of aldermen, and it was also necessary for these two bodies to provide the funds. On a report submitted by the comptroller, $13,250 was transferred from the department of charities and from the bridge department to provide salaries for the mayor's new secretaries and for other additional expenditures by the mayor. E. Stagg Whitin was paid at the rate of $4,000 per year until it was decided to dispense with his services, a protest having been lodged with the municipal commission against his appointment by fifth grade clerks on the preferred list, Coffey and Curtis. The municipal commission ordered an examination for the position of assistant secretary to the mayor after the request for exemption was denied by the State Commission, and 143 applications were filed. Twenty-three of these applicants passed the experience test, when the examination was canceled. The municipal commission spent time and money preparing for the examination, and the applicants, including many newspaper men, devoted considerable energy preparing for test before it was called off. The refusal of the State Commission to exempt these two places resulted in saving several thousand dollars in salaries, and caused the mayor to suddenly realize that he could get along without the assistants he so anxiously desired. (*Proof that he did not need what he said he needed.*)

Provisional Appointments Under Municipal Civil Service Rule XII, Paragraph 3

From information furnished the State Civil Service Commission by the Municipal Civil Service Commission, during the month of September, 1914, it appears that there were forty-five provisional appointees holding positions at that time, as shown by last payroll submitted, who had been designated during the year 1913. These employees held the positions of bookkeeper, chemist, assistant chemist, junior chemist, finger print expert, inspector of sewer construction, probation officer, assistant pharmacists, steward and topographical draftsman. The appointments date from March 24th for finger print expert to December 24th, for bookkeeper. Lists for many of these positions were not established until late in the year 1914, and the provisional appointees continued in office in most cases for a year or more, or until appointed from the eligible list or superseded by other appointees. In two cases, however, lists have not been established, namely, chemist, department of health, and steward, department of charities. The three persons who were appointed provisionally to the position of chemist, May 27, July 18, and December 9, 1913, respectively, each at a salary of $1,200 per annum, we assume are still in office, as the commission is informed by the chief payroll clerk, under date of January 15, 1915, that "up to the present time there has been no list promulgated to fill vacancies for this position."

One provisional appointment was made July 27, 1913, to the position of steward, department of charities, salary $960 per annum. The State Commission is advised that no list had been promulgated for this position up to January 15, 1915, and that the provisional appointee "is still retained in the service." It appears, therefore, that the chemist, who was appointed provisionally in the department of health, May 27, 1913, has served approximately one year and eight months, and that the steward, who was appointed provisionally in the department of charities, July 27, 1913, has served approximately one year and six months, notwithstanding the fact that the provisions of section 15, subdivision 1, of the Civil Service Law, provides that "provisional appointment shall not continue for a longer period than two months."

During the year 1914, 345 appointments were made under the provisions of civil service rule 12, paragraph 3, covering about seventy-five different kinds or groups of positions. In a great majority of these cases, the lists were not established within the required period of sixty days, particularly in the cases of bookkeeper, inspector of plumbing, hospital clerk (department of health), nurse (department of health), finger print expert, assistant photographer, inspector of foods, trade instructor, auto truck driver, pathological chemist, gardener, and many others. With the exception of the provisional appointees to the position of finger print expert, list for which position was established September 23, 1914, and subsequently canceled, provisional appointees who exceeded the statutory limitation ranged from sixty-three days for the position of nurse, department of health, to 321 days, for the position of bookkeeper, finance department.

There are still other positions which were filled by provisional appointment during the year 1914, for which lists had not been established up to January 15, 1915. Among these are the following:

Postion	Provisional Appointment
Inspector of Fire Alarm Boxes (Fire Department)	June 19, 1914.
Morgue Keeper (Department of Charities)	March 16, 1914.
Probation Officer	April 16 and June 22, 1914.
Lumber Inspector, Department of Docks and Ferries	April 17, 1914.
Chemist, Department of Health	April 17, 1914.
Junior Chemist	June 8, 1914.
Resident Physician, Department of Charities	April 25 and May 1, 1914.
Resident Physician, Department of Correction	May 13, 1914.
Salary and Grade Examiner	June 29 and July 2, 1914.
Inspector, Board of Water Supply	July 21 and August 19, 1914.
Gymnasium Attendant, Public Recreation Commission	August 11, 1914.
Superintendent of Asphalt Repairing Plant	August 1, 1914.
Supervising Inspector, Borough President, Manhattan	August 19, 1914.

The periods of provisional employment vary, the longest being for position of morgue keeper, department of charities, covering approximately ten months.

In this connection, it seems pertinent that we briefly discuss the so-called "special certificate," which was prepared by the municipal civil service commission in the year 1903, and which has from time to come, been attached to payrolls. The certificate reads as follows:

"I hereby certify that this payroll has been examined and in so far as it applies to .... for services rendered as .... from .... to .... is for a period subsequent to such time as the municipal civil service commission could attach its regular certificate; that, under the law and rules made in pursuance of law, no appointment for the period mentioned could be made, that the services of the person named were immediately necessary; that at the time these services were rendered, no eligible list for the position in question could be or was certified by the municipal civil service commission to the appointing officer to fill such position, and pending the establishment of an eligible list for temporary or permanent appointment, the payroll of the person above named for services rendered, is owing to the peculiar and unusual circumstances certified by the municipal civil service commission, upon the grounds that the decisions of the courts require payment of employees of the city who have performed work for it and when no certification of an eligible list could be made to fill the position.

MUNICIPAL CIVIL SERVICE COMMISSION,

By ....,

Assistant Secretary."

The certificate is used in order to permit the payment of compensation to persons appointed under the circumstances mentioned therein, for services which they had actually rendered to the city, and its use followed an opinion rendered by the corporation counsel to the municipal civil service commission, in reply to an inquiry as to its authority to certify accounts for services rendered after the sixty-days period permitted by the statute. The adoption and use of this "special certificate" must encourage delay in holding examinations and promulgating lists in cases where provisional appointments have been made. We hardly believe that the corporation counsel ever contemplated the use of the certificate except in most extreme cases, and to have a stamp ready at hand to place upon the payroll of any person whose salary could not otherwise be certified, is a *misuse of the privilege.* This is especially true when the stamp is used on payrolls of provisional appointees who have never been examined, when apparently there was no reason for delaying their examination.

Provisional Appointments to Positions to be Filled After Promotion Examinations

During the course of the investigation, it was discovered that it was the practice of the Municipal Civil Service Commission to accept provisional appointments to positions to be filled *after* promotion examination. The only authority for this procedure is found in section 15, subdivision 1, of the Civil Service Law, which provides for filling positions in certain cases without competitive examination. We consider that the construction given by the municipal commission to said provision of the statute, is *unwarranted.* Nowhere in the State, other than in the city of New York, where the Civil Service Law and rules apply, are provisional appointments accepted preliminary to promotion examination. Even the promotion rule governing the New York city service does not refer in any way to provisional appointments. In fact the promotion rule seems to run contrary to this practice. Section 1 of rule XIV, which relates to promotions, provides that "vacancies in positions above the lowest grade in any part of competitive class * * * shall be filled by promotion, based so far as practicable, on *competitive tests.*"

Section 2 of the rule, provides that "examinations for promotion shall be ordered as often as may be necessary to *meet or anticipate* the needs of the higher grades."

Section 3 provides that no person shall be eligible for promotion "who lacks any of the preliminary requirements for original entrance to the position to be filled."

Under no logical construction of the Civil Service Law in the judgment of the State Commission can temporary or provisional selection be made for positions which are required to be filled by promotion through competitive examination. The spirit, if not the letter of the law, is contrary to such procedure, as it gives an appointing officer undue advantage in designating presumably the person whose promotion is desired; and while giving the appointee opportunity to familiarize himself with the duties of the position to which promotion is sought, acts as a deterrent to other candidates as well as a delay to the holding of the examination.

Rating Sheets

Civil Service Commissions are frequently criticised for methods which seem mysterious or difficult to understand. Methods of examination or of rating papers which are not easy of comprehension should be avoided in order to satisfy candidates and the public at large, that everything is open and above-board; contrary methods undermine confidence and weaken the merit system in the eyes of the people.

The Municipal Civil Service Commission in rating papers does not put the credit allowed answers on the papers themselves, but a "rating-sheet" is used to which one must refer in order to understand the ratings; this is unsatisfactory to the candidates who very naturally wish to know exactly the amount of credit allowed for each answer.

A competitor reviewing his examination papers sees only the lump mark given for the entire paper, but if there are ten questions, he naturally desires to see the rating allowed each question; this "rating-sheet" system should, in our opinion, be abandoned for the reason indicated above, and for the further reason that it increases the possibility of error in computing averages.

Furthermore, a "make-up" sheet should be attached to each set of papers showing exactly how much the competitor is credited in each subject of the examination, weights allowed, and the computations necessary in computing the average. This system of marking each answer in plain figures and computations on a make-up sheet for each competitor is the system used by the United States Civil Service Commission, and the New York State Civil Service Commission, and should be adopted by the Municipal Civil Service Commission.

"Experts" at a Cost of One Million Dollars in 1914

The municipal commission permitted the appointment during the year 1914 of 196 persons under rule 12, paragraph 8, which provides for the employment of "experts" whose compensation and period of service cannot be determined in advance. Among these was Delos F. Wilcox, formerly head of the Franchise Bureau of the Public Service Commission. Mr. Wilcox was appointed by Mayor Mitchel "in connection with regulating the rates at which private water companies shall deliver water to customers in Greater New York."

Mr. Wilcox testified (p. 6403) that he organized a staff of engineers in the Water Department to begin an appraisal of the private water plants from whom the people of Queens and part of Brooklyn purchase water. He continued as "expert" 12-8 from July 9 to October 15, 1914, and was then appointed Deputy Commissioner of the Department of Water Supply, Gas and Electricity, to continue the work of appraisal. His salary as Deputy Commissioner is $6,000 per year. As Chief of the Bureau of Franchises of the Public Service Commission his salary was $4,000.

Under Rule 12–8, the Municipal Commission permitted the appointment of detectives and others at a total cost to the city of many thousands of dollars during the year 1914. With all the 12–6 appointments the total cost of "expert" service in 1914 *approximates* $1,000,000.

Laborers (Non-Competitive) Assigned to Competitive Positions

Many persons are concerned with this matter. We received numerous complaints, and found that many complaints were filed with the local commission. A large part of Examiner Fuld's time, during 1914, has been occupied investigating these complaints and complaints regarding employees working outside of their titles (see his testimony, p. 6783, etc.), which indicates how general throughout the departments was this kind of violation during the year 1914.

The first witness on this subject was Edward J. McInerney, President of the Interborough Association of eligible male attendants, and a clerk in the employ of the city (p. 2997). His testimony showed a serious condition in the Department of Parks, Dock Department and other branches of the city government. Laborers were acting as attendants in public comfort stations and in some cases were unable to understand or speak the English language, or to give proper directions.

Laborers in the Dock Department were doing clerical and other work, not appropriate to their title, and other laborers were acting as janitors. This commission pressed the matter in the hearings, and as a result of that pressure, the Municipal Civil Service Commission has stiffened up and considerable improvement has resulted. *There are still many violations in this direction.*

On principle and in fact, the spirit of civil service (which is the real protection of the law) may be more seriously injured in those humble places than in higher ones.

The practice of holding promotion examinations from *labor positions* to *competitive positions* is questionable as it does an injustice to those who would otherwise have an opportunity to compete for the higher grade places.

An amendment to the rules to change this procedure is recommended.

(On the main question, see testimony of Birdseye 3024, McDonald 3034, Fuld 3390 and 6783, McInerney 3396, Vesce 5926, McNally 6153, Dock laborers 3462 to 3499, etc.)

Monitors.

Robert W. Belcher, Secretary of the Municipal Civil Service Commission, was formerly Secretary of the Civil Service Reform Association, and as such he transmitted the protests of that organization against the conduct of the former commissioners who retained certain individuals employed as monitors to do clerical and investigating work. On this the association made a strong point, and the letters of protest were emphatic. Mr. Belcher became secretary of the Municipal Commission last May, and the new commissioners practised *exactly the same violation of law.* The Civil Service Reform Association did *not* protest, and Mr. Belcher as secretary of the Commission, *made the certifications on the payrolls stating that said monitors had not been doing work inappropriate to their titles, when in fact they had been doing that very thing.*

It is not to be wondered at that other departments come to regard the Civil Service Law as a convenience, *to be used when it serves their purposes and to be ignored when it does not.* (See testimony of Secretary Birdseye (page 426) which shows that the work of monitors is to attend examinations, watch the candidates, distribute and collect papers, and aid the examiners on the day of examination.)

On January 5, 1914, Chief Examiner Ireland wrote the Municipal Commission that monitors were employed in doing clerical or quasi-clerical work. This report was referred to Commissioner James, who reported to President Moskowitz *that it was illegal and should not be allowed.* He suggested that the secretary (then Mr. Spencer) try to formulate a plan for changing their titles —

or possibly to continue one or two monitors and dispense with the others as clerks. On January 26, 1914, the president, the secretary and the chief examiner were appointed a committee to report on the matter. The Committee did not report, but Mr. Spencer gave the commissioners a list of the monitors and a detail of their work. He recommended that their positions be made competitive. *No further action was taken.*

Evidence showed that a number of monitors, some of whom had been with the commission several years, were really doing work not appropriate to the title. *Following written announcement that the State Commission was about to examine* the local commission *these monitors were all dropped,* on September 5, 1914. (The preliminary inspection began September 8th.)

The provision of the statute which was violated is section 14 of the Civil Service Law, which provides "that no person shall be appointed or employed under any title not appropriate to the duties to be performed." The former secretary, Mr. Spencer, says (page 450) he told the commissioners it was a violation of law.

Payrolls for July and August, 1914, are shown in the record (page 486) and President Moskowitz's signature is on it with that of Mr. Belcher. Mr. Belcher testified (page 490) and admitted that the certificate signed by him was *not true* (page 493); he said he had followed an old custom. *He admitted that previously on behalf of the Civil Service Reform Association, he had written the local commission in condemnation of the illegal practice.*

"Q. (page 499.) Do you mean to say that as an official you would sign an incorrect statement, just in order that people may be paid? A. That is the way the statement was signed. Q. Of course you having a good purpose, it might be construed as a precedent that would be followed by other officials with a *bad* purpose. Did you ever think of that? A. Yes, but the fact is, *it is done in every city department.*"

Here is the excuse for the evil — *to be prevalent in the departments* — and which, as shown in the Department of Public Works, *is a powerful means of working injustice and wrong. Their example was right in the Municipal Civil Service Commission, and it did not reform until this State probe began to work; then it reformed suddenly.* Other reforms in that commission and other departments have accompanied the investigation, so that *in the improving of civil service conditions the investigation justified itself as it went along.*

Mr. Belcher said (page 526): " *Whatever I did, I understood I was carrying out the policy of the commission.*"

The answer of the commission to many of the specifications of violation of plain provisions of the civil service law, is that they are inherited by this administration; so was its own monitor system. There was more need of attention to these plain violations of law than there was *to meddling with physical examinations that left them worse than before. They let their own violations run till the moment of the day of judgment. They have withheld action on flagrant violations revealed to them in the hearings, such as those in the Department of Public Works, even putting through untruthful payrolls.*

Small wonder is it that in some public offices the employees tell us they have lost all faith in the law and in the purpose of the local commission to enforce it, when its enforcement would annoy friends. The *stopping of a few payrolls would quickly end the general violation of law.*

The Case of Samuel Brock

In the case of Samuel Brock, executive clerk in the office of the president of Queens Borough, the municipal commission deliberately prepared the way for him and certified his payroll for the month of January, 1914, at the rate of $2,250 a year as fourth grade clerk, when *no such position existed* in the office of the Queens Borough president. The commission also accepted Brock's own certification to that payroll when the payroll clerk, Miss McGee, *declined to sign it.* Brock's payroll for the succeeding month, February, was accepted and certified by the municipal commission at the rate of $4,000 per year, though the position of executive clerk at that salary was *not* created by the board of aldermen until February 11th, and Brock was *ineligible* for emergency or provisional appointment until July 9th succeeding.

Brock, who was a fourth grade clerk in the office of the comptroller, was appointed secretary to the Borough of Queens at $4,000 per year in March, 1913. His salary as fourth grade clerk was $2,250 per annum. His term as secretary to the borough expired on December 31, 1913. He continued in the employ of the president of the Borough of Queens, his position of secretary to the borough being filled after December 31, 1913, by another incumbent. Brock was therefore without a position in the office of the borough president in Queens, and though he worked in the office as clerk from then until February 11th, when the position of executive clerk was created by the board of aldermen, there seems to be no legal ground for his service or justification for compensation during that period.

The payrolls of Mr. Brock for the months of January and February, 1914, show that he was paid at the rate of $2,250 per year for the entire month of January and at the rate of $4,000 per year for February. It was on the same date, February 11, 1914, that the position of executive clerk in the Borough of Queens was established by the board of aldermen, *that the municipal civil service commission amended clause* 3 *of rule* 14 to apply to the case of a civil service employee "*appointed*" to an exempt position, restoring such employee "either to the position originally held by him or to any position to which transfer could be made therefrom."

Brock testified that his reinstatement to the position of fourth grade clerk in Queens occurred on January 9, 1914, under a ruling of the municipal commission (p. 2030). Brock's payroll for the month of January, which he himself certified, is divided into two periods by the municipal commission, the first period from January 1 to 8, the second from January 9 to 31. Both periods of employment are certified by the municipal commission, and the first period is noted in writing and so specially certified. The amount of the payroll is $187.50, covering the entire month at the rate of $2,250 per year. In connection with this fact, the testimony of Lawrence A. Byrne, chief payroll clerk of the Municipal Civil Service Commission and of Frank A. Spencer, then secretary of the commission, is explanatory. Mr. Byrne testified (p. 5935) that from January 1st to 8th, the municipal commission approved Mr. Brock's appointment under Rule 12, paragraph 4 and that Brock was reinstated as fourth grade clerk on January 9th. His appointment as executive clerk at $4,000 per annum was *approved* by the commission for the entire month of February, in spite of the fact as previously stated, the position was not officially created until February 11th and that Brock was ineligible for appointment. Mr. Byrne also testified that as fourth grade clerk in the finance department, Mr. Brock was receiving $2,100 per year (p. 5937).

Mr. Spencer testified (p. 3039) that while he was secretary of the municipal commission, the president asked him several times " what could be done in the Brock matter," that he advised the president that an appointment under rule 12, paragraph 5, exempting Brock as " executive clerk " was *improper.* He said (p. 3040): " The President then asked me whether he could not be appointed from the position of fourth grade clerk to this position of executive clerk, he having been appointed in the meantime to a position as clerk at $2,250 in the borough president's office. To that position he was eligible at $2,250, he having been a $2,250 clerk within a year in another department. I told the president in response to that, that *I did not see how a promotion examination could be given him because he had not been three months in the department as required under the promotion rule."* * * * " I think it is six months, in the department, yes. As a result of that there was no promotion examination held at that time. I remember telling the president — Brock had asked for it." He said that Brock was ineligible for provisional appointment as " executive clerk " prior to July 9th, because he was ineligible for promotion prior to that date. The records of the municipal commission and the testimony of Payroll Clerk Byrne show that Brock was certified as " executive clerk " and drew pay at $4,000 per year for the month of February.

The resolution of the board of aldermen of February 11th, establishing the position of " executive clerk " in Queens at $4,000 per year, shows that Borough President Connolly had a *particular appointee* in mind when the position was established. The minutes of the board of aldermen read (p. 6308): " That President Connolly informed the committee that this official was needed particularly in connection with the establishment of the maintenance of a cost data system of records requiring the services of an experienced and highly capable man such *as he proposed to appoint."* Brock himself testified (p. 2042), that there was an eligible list for fifth grade clerk (the grade for executive clerkship) in existence in Queens (p. 2042); that one person was on the eligible list and " Mr. Connolly did not care to appoint that man." That person was Harry K. Vought, who appeared as a witness before the State Commission on January 7, 1915. Mr. Vought had advanced in the service in Queens for more than ten years. He testified that he took an examination in August, 1913, for fifth grade clerkship in Queens, because the chief clerk had died and there was a vacancy in that grade (p. 5713). No appointment was made to the chief clerkship and the position was abolished by the board of aldermen on February 11th succeeding, when they created the new fifth grade clerkship to which Mr. Brock was appointed first provisionally, then permanently. Mr. Vought and another fourth grade clerk in Queens entered the examination for fifth grade clerkship with Brock in October, 1914, but neither Vought, nor the other candidate, Murray, qualified. Brock was the only candidate who passed the examination, having held the position since February and drawn the pay for that month.

The testimony shows that the examination for the position of fifth grade clerk in Queens borough was delayed until Brock became eligible by the lapse of six months from January 9, when he was officially reinstated as fourth grade clerk. The examination was ordered by the municipal commission on July 9, exactly six months after Brock's reinstatement, and the earliest date on which he became eligible. Some of the questions in the examination were written to fit the duties of the office of executive clerk which Brock had held in violation of the rules since February 1, with the approval of the municipal commission. Brock was asked (p. 5396) why he did not reimburse the city for the extra month which he received after January 1, as fifth grade clerk. "Because," he said, *" The city never asked me for it."*

The testimony quoted above was given on January 6, 1915. On November 5, 1914 (p. 2026) Mr. Brock had testified that the

" $4,000 rate started early in the year, and under the ruling of the Civil Service Commission, made on the report by the secretary, which provided for a reinstatement into the service instead of another process which we thought was proper, there was a period there when the salary of $4,000 was paid." He said: " Then upon a report which ruled that I was *not* eligible until six months after January 9, which was the date fixed as having been my date of reinstatement, there was a question as to whether this process of reinstatement was a correct one at all. We had another idea over there, but this was the first time I ever saw this process worked out this way, and it was a matter of judgment as to which was the proper procedure, and it was simply a ruling of the commission that I was not entitled to draw the salary from the early part of the year, due entirely to their ruling as to my method of coming back into the classified service."

Mr. Brock was asked about his personal relation with President Moskowitz when he was re-examined on January 5, 1913. He said: " I never knew him as a personal friend * * * nothing more than to meet him in the restaurant and say " How do you do?" He visited him in his home once, he said, and stayed there about twenty minutes.

Mr. Brock finally acknowledged that he walked with President Moskowitz from the latter's office in the Municipal building to the Henry Street Settlement and then to the president's house, but denied that he told anyone he had supper there. He then acknowledged that he had taken dinner with Dr. Moskowitz in a public restaurant with other people, *several times,* and that he had sat at a table with him *while this examination was pending.* He said he did not recall what he talked to him about but that he knew he did not discuss the examination.

Lewis Mayers, civil service examiner who prepared the questions in the competitive examination in which Brock alone qualified, was asked during the examination of Brock if the data which he received from the Commissioner of Public Works in Queens, with reference to the duties of the position of "executive clerk" was incorporated in the questions used in the examination. He said (p. 5403): " It is very difficult to say whether the data was incorporated. Of course some consideration was had for the duties of the position in making up the questions; *that was necessary.*"

William J. Murray, fourth grade clerk in Queens, who took the examination for fifth grade clerk with Brock and Harry K. Vought on October 9, 1914, testified (page 5355):

"Q. Do you consider that a large part of the questions were written to conform with the duties of the office that Mr. Brock was filling? A. *Well they were more of an executive character than one would meet as a fifth grade clerk.* He said that had he occupied the place Brock did, possibly he could have answered the questions more accurately."

Harry K. Vought, the other candidate in the examination with Brock, who failed with Murray, testified on January 7 (p. 5718):

"Q. Were some of the questions in the second examination written around the duties that Mr. Brock was performing for the six months previous, or for several months previous to the examination? A. *I think so: yes, sir.*

Q. What part of the questions were written around the duties fulfilled by Mr. Brock during that time? A. *As regards executive ability and office management and such things as that.*"

In testifying with reference to the delay in calling the competitive examination for the position, former Secretary Spencer said (p. 3041): "I told the President I did not think he could afford to stand the criticism of *delaying a promotion examination for Brock. Brock would not be qualified until about July, and to delay a promotion examination would no doubt cause criticism.* That is about the last I heard of it." He said that conversation with Dr. Moskowitz was in January or February, and that the examination was called in July.

At the time Brock was appointed fifth grade clerk in Queens provisionally, there was a preferred list for fifth grade clerkship in existence containing the names of said Philip Coffey and Claude Curtis who has been dropped from the labor bureau of the municipal commission when the bureau was abolished. Before Brock was appointed temporarily on July 9, though he received the salary of the office for the month of February, the municipal commission obtained an opinion from the corporation counsel enabling them *to set aside the preferred list* and appoint Brock. Coffey is an exempt fireman and has brought suit for reinstatement against the city. The list for fifth grade clerkship in Queens, containing the name of Harry K. Vought, *was in existence when Brock was appointed.*

PAYROLL OF JOSEPH T. WILLIAMS AS "EXPERT" APPROVED FOR MORE THAN TWO MONTHS WHEN HE WAS INELIGIBLE FOR EMPLOYMENT.

Joseph T. Williams was permitted through the neglect of the Municipal Commission to draw two and a half months pay from August 17, 1914, at the rate of $100 per month before the commission discovered that the appointee was not qualified for employment under rule 12, paragraph 6, under which he served. Mr. Williams was at work during that period in the Domestic Relations Bureau of the Charities Department and his name appears on the payrolls of the department for August, September and October, according to the testimony of Commissioner Keogh. Mr. Williams testified that he also received $100 per month during that period from the Association for Improving the Condition of the Poor, making his total compensation two hundred dollars a month, which he is now receiving from the charitable organization.

The Municipal Civil Service Commission had no roster card showing Mr. Williams' employment by the city, though under the rules, a roster card must be kept of every person drawing pay from the city of New York. After Mr. Williams' name appeared on three monthly payrolls, the Municipal Commission decided that Mr. Williams was not eligible for exception and removed his name from the roll. This action was taken more than two months *after* the investigation of the Municipal Commission by the State body was begun. Mr. Williams testified that while working for the city he sent a copy of his reports looking to a "reorganization" of the management of the Domestic Relations Bureau, to the A. I. C. P., the private charitable organization which paid half his salary during that period, and all of it subsequently. Mr. Williams was employed by that organization (p. 6400) prior to drawing pay from the city.

Commissioner Keogh, in explaining the Williams appointment, said (p. 6409): "Mr. Williams was paid for two months and a half. There was no roster card, because he was never appointed, but he did the work from the 17th of August and was paid by the city for the two and a half months' work that he did."

President Neu: "He was paid because he did the work?"

Commissioner Keogh: "It came in with all the others, under the 12–6, the forty-five or forty-six (charity examiners in the charities department), and it was approved by the payroll clerk, although his name had never been approved, under 12–6 and his application when it came in here, was finally disapproved and his name was deducted from the payroll from that time on."

Commissioner Wolff: "You mean he was working before your board acted on his case?"

Commissioner Keogh: "Before that 12–6 was approved."

Commissioner Wolff: "And he was working for two and a half months before there was any action by your board?"

Commissioner Keogh: "Enough to pass his payroll for those two and a half months, that was passed."

Labor Bureau

The municipal civil service commission showed that it was able to play at practical politics, though it was against the wishes of one of the commissioners.

A part of the established system of the Commission was a very efficient labor bureau. It was organized about fifteen years ago by the veteran secretary Mr. Spencer, who was an expert in civil service matters. Associated with him early was Philip Coffey and later Claude F. Curtis. These men *made* the labor bureau, which was considered to be a model, and Mr. Coffey was called upon by other cities as an expert. The labor service is noncompetitive; it provides nearly one-third of the city employees. In numbers it fluctuates and changes suddenly at times, for in emergencies and on occasions great numbers of men are hired or discharged. It deals with large numbers of uneducated, unintelligent and unskilled men, and physical and practical requirements have to be administered in a way of its own by persons accustomed to the class of unskilled workers. Tact and experience are necessary to manage the applicants; care is required in keeping and maintaining the records in order that men shall have their civil service rights and that the city shall be protected against claims which sometimes are of large amounts. Specialized care in this particular is likely to save the city much more than the amount expended in salaries for the bureau. There is such a difference between the competitive class and the noncompetitive labor class that efficient management in the long run requires separation.

It so happened that these men who had built up this work and had become recognized as efficient experts were Democrats. The commissioners had the right to discharge the secretary and they did so, at the same time expressing their appreciation of his character and ability; but Coffey and Curtis were within the supposed protection of Civil Service Law. It was not possible to dispose of them without proven charges, so it was worked on the ground of *economy*. Some young man connected with the bureau of municipal research and who had no practical connection with labor, "poked around" for a day or two and made an "efficiency" report on which the commissioners took action for a *consolidation of this noncompetitive labor bureau with the competitive work and records,* and they abolished the bureau and dropped Mr. Coffey and Mr. Curtis after their years of faithful service, without making any real effort to place them in other positions, compelling them to seek redress for reinstatement at law on the ground that they are veterans. This action was based on a claim of saving $8,000 a year in salaries, which on examination and proper allowances comes down to $5,900. *The city, however, is likely to lose much more in the long run through law suits in which its rights are not conserved by the care and attention which the labor bureau exercised in those matters.*

One commissioner was opposed to the ousting of Coffey and Curtis and several commissioners of former administrations who were politically opposite to these men appeared and expressed their *disapproval of the abolition of the bureau and their confidence in the men who were dropped.* These included Mr. Creelman, Mr.

Welling and Mr. Gallagher. Corporation Counsel Polk testified to his confidence in Mr. Coffey and to the *effort he made to save him in the service.* It appeared that a well known politician called Gene Driscoll had notified these men that they would have to go unless they went to the city hall and arranged with " John." Mr. Coffey answered and said that he did not need to see anyone, that he could stand on his record, but he said sadly, he found he was mistaken. According to the testimony, after delivering one of these remarks in the hallway of the municipal building, Gene said he was on his way to see " Henry." Subpoenas were issued for Driscoll but he was not found, and though the testimony was published he never appeared to contradict it. Mr. Sheehan, a clerk, was called by the local civil service commission, and he admitted that he was sent by Dr. Moskowitz to "collaborate " with Mr. Coffey, *but really to learn the business, to learn the things that Mr. Coffey had in his head* (so that Coffey's work could be taken by Sheehan after Coffey's departure). It is evident that Sheehan is the man who is to fill Coffey's place. (Sheehan was the teacher of Driscoll's children.)

Mr. Coffey and Mr. Curtis being placed on the preferred list had hopes of being appointed to a vacancy in the Queens county borough president's office, but that was filled by Samuel Brock, above mentioned, the provisional appointee who was nursed along to a permanent appointment. So these skilled and faithful city employees are out of the public service on account of politics, and those who point out the injustice will be accused by the insiders of being moved by political spite in pointing *to the evasion of civil services principles by the Civil Service Commission itself.*

But if the civil service be not maintained in strength and spirit by reformers, who shall preach to the practical politicians? Example teaches, and for the sake of that example, in such a municipal administration as the present, *it is a pity that so questionable an act was done, and that such an indefensible piece of spoils-politics should have been performed.*

Delayed Examinations

The work of any civil service commission is largely determined by the number and character of competitive examinations and the promptness with which lists are established, in order to enable appointing officers to fill places without being obliged to make temporary or provisional appointments.

There have been great delays in examinations for the municipal service, some of which have been caused by the attempt to get experts in various subjects not only to suggest questions but also to manage the examination. Men may be experts in particular subjects and still lack the practical experience of examiners — which supplies a special tact in ascertaining the knowledge of candidates and reporting the same expeditioulsy.

President Moskowitz was asked about his effort to "elevate" the examination for "examiner of charitable institutions," for which purpose he secured the organization of a committee of "social workers." He testified (p. 6532): "Then the subcommittee was appointed to consider the question, the problem of the examination. This subcommittee consisted of Mrs. John M. Glenn, Mr. Sidney Goldstein and Dr. Edmond Butler, of the Catholic Home Bureau. They then sent those questions to the Commission. I submitted those questions to Miss Upshaw (examiner), and the idea being that if necessary the Commission might appoint an expert either from among those three or somebody else in co-operation with the regular examiners who give this examination. It was thought best after a while that we have our own people who would do this work and we did not use any experts for the preparation of those questions, and in fact our own examiners thought that the questions were *not practical,* and used their own questions, that is the whole — that is the story of this whole matter."

"Q. (P. 6534) All questions submitted by the experts were rejected? A. *They were rejected by our examiners.* Our examiners did not — they thought they would make out their own questions and they made out their own questions."

Examiner Lewis Mayers testified that two of the questions used in the examination for "Examiner of Charitable Institutions" were prepared by him. "Q. (p. 6511) What became of the questions that they submitted, or were submitted to you and the rest of the examiners? A. Miss Upshaw showed them to me and we looked them over and decided they were *absolutely valueless for the purpose,* because of very patent defects in the way they had been made up, because they were not calculated to bring out the type of answer that we desired, and I discarded that paper entirely. * * * Q. Well, the questions in the examination were not repeated in the questions in the examination, were they? A. I do not recall anything on that paper that appeared in the questions in the examination."

From figures obtained from the municipal commission, it appears that the number of examinations held from January 1, 1913, to January 1, 1914, was 418, with total number of 24,246 candidates. The number of examinations held by the present commission, from January 1, 1915, was 336, with 21,348 candidates. A comparison of these figures shows a *decrease* in the number of examinations of approximately 20 per cent., with a *decrease* in the number of candidates of about 13 per cent. During the same period the number of employees of the commission *increased.*

That unusual delays occur in holding examinations after the same are ordered, and (when held) in completing the ratings and promulgating the lists, is shown by the following examples:

Examination	Ordered	Held	List promulgated
Yiddish interpreter	Oct. 29, 1913	Mar. 26, 1914	Dec. 9, 1914
Italian interpreter	Oct. 29, 1913	Mar. 24, 1914	Dec. 2, 1914
Statistician (Gr. E.)	Oct. 22, 1913	Mar. 17, and 19, 1914	May 13, 1914
Hospital clerk	Oct. 6, 1913	May 4, and 5, 1914	Aug. 10, 1914
Chemist and bacteriologist	Aug. 20, 1913	April 23, 1914	May 13, 1914
Laboratory assistant	Nov. 12, 1913	May 29, 1914	Aug. 5, 1914
Police matron	Sept. 17, 1913	July 7, 1914	Oct. 21, 1914
Photographer (X-ray) (re-ordered by present Commission April 1, 1914)	Dec. 15, 1913	Aug. 14, 1914	Nov. 25, 1914
Civil Service examiner (engineer)	Dec. 23, 1913	July 14, and Nov. 10, 1914	Dec. 9, 1914
Finger print expert	Dec. 23, 1913	July 8, 1914	Sept. 23, 1914

The present local commission ordered and held examinations and promulgated lists as follows:

Examination	Ordered	Held	List promulgated
Telephone operator	Jan. 17, 1914	Mar. 31, 1914	July 8, 1914
Engineer chemist	Feb. 4, 1914	July 1, 1914	Aug. 7, 1914
Fireman (volunteer)	Feb. 18, 1914	May 29, 1914	Aug. 5, 1914
Attendant (female)	Jan. 7, 1914	July 2, 1914	Oct. 7, 1914
Automobile engineman	Mar. 4, 1914	Aug. 13, 1914	Dec. 2, 1914
Bookkeeper (third grade)	Feb. 25, 1914	July 9, 1914	Dec. 2, 1914
Superintendent Municipal Sanatorium	April 1, 1914	July 23, 1914	Sept. 23, 1914
Draftsman, Grade C	Mar. 11, 1914	June 23, 1914	Sept. 28, 1914
Photographer	Jan. 7, 1914	July 30, 1914	Sept. 16, 1914
Examiner of charitable institutions	April 29, 1914	Sept. 24, and Nov. 24, 1914	Dec. 31, 1914

The time elapsed between the date examinations were ordered and the date the lists resulting therefrom were promulgated, vary from 165 days in the case of firemen (volunteer) to 1 year and 41 days for the position of Yiddish interpreter.

From testimony of Assistant Examiner Murray of the municipal commission, given near the close of the hearing, it appears that since our investigation was commenced a new plan has been devised for expediting examinations. It consists of the keeping of a book in the nature of a timetable with blank columns for the various steps in the examination to be filled out as they are taken. Strange as it may seem, there was no provision for doing this natural thing until recently, when it became necessary to overcome the *evil of delay* which our Commission has complained of since last fall. Mr. Murray also testified that *more has been accomplished in the last three months of the year* 1914 *than during the previous nine months.* It is to be hoped that the stimulus of our investigation will last.

Late in our investigation Assistant Chief Examiner Upshaw gave a list of examinations that have been pending for six months or over. The records of the municipal civil service commissions show the following open competitive examinations ordered January 1, 1914, to July 15, 1914, the eligible list for which have *not* been promulgated:

Examination	Date Ordered
Supervising Nurse	February 4. 1914.
Chemist, Food and Drugs	March 4, 1914.
Engineer Inspector, Architectural, Grades "C" and "D"	April 29, 1914.
Resident Physician, Grade 2	April 29, 1914.
Salary and Grade Examiner	May 6, 1914.
Gardner	May 13, 1914.
Temporary Clerk	June 3, 1914.
Director, Bureau of Food Inspection	June 10, 1914.
Supervising Inspector, Grade 5	June 10, 1914.
Inspector of Meters and Water Consumption, Grade 2	June 17, 1914.
Inspector of Carpentry and Masonry,	June 17, 1914.
Grade 2	June 17, 1914.
Court Stenographer, Grades 4 and 5	June 17, 1914.
Electrician	June 17. 1914.
Examiner, Law Department	July 1, 1914.
Playground and Gymnasium Attendant	June 24, 1914.
Fireman	July 8, 1914.
Topographical Draughtsman, Grade "C"	July 8, 1914.
Tabulating Machine Operator	July 8, 1914.
Farm Instructor	July 15, 1914.

Examination.	Date Ordered
Investigator	July 15, 1914.
Steward	July 15, 1914.
Secretary to Committee on Social Welfare	July 15, 1914.
Secretary to Committee on Markets	July 15, 1914.
Superintendent, Municipal Lodging House	July 15, 1914.

From the testimony of Miss Upshaw, it appears that the examiners in the year 1913 passed on 30,000 papers left over by the former commission and did their regular work also. (They were not then handicapped by *fads* and *fancies,* including special " expert examiners.")

Free Employment Bureau

Age Limit for Superintendent Removed by Municipal Commission

The municipal commission advertised an examination for superintendent of the Free Employment Bureau in November, 1914. Sixty-three applicants were filed in response to this advertisement, and one application was received from an individual residing in Boston, named Walter L. Sears. The application of Sears was rejected, and he was barred from entering an examination because he was over age, the age limit of candidates being fixed at fifty years, and so stated in the advertisement. Among those who filed applications to enter the examination were the managers and directors of private and quasi-public employment agencies in the city of New York, including Willis Hawley, director of the Employment Bureau of the Y. M. C. A. in Brooklyn, and Sarah J. Atwood, director of the Atwood Employment Agency in Manhattan. Both of these applicants were considered particularly competent for service as head of an employment bureau by Commissioner of Licenses George H. Bell, whose jurisdiction includes supervision over the city's free employment bureau and private employment agencies. (See Mr. Bell's testimony, page 5144).

The fact that Mr. Sears was a non-resident of the city also barred him from employment in New York city until such disability was removed as provided in the ordinance by presentation of evidence that no one in New York could be found to properly perform the services required.

License Commissioner Bell testified that he had gone to Boston to consult Mr. Sears about accepting the position of superintendent of the Free Employment Bureau. He said that he had inquired diligently in New York for "almost a year" to find someone who could "do the job." Mr. Bell made it a point that he wanted someone who had had experience in running a public employment bureau (p. 5136) and for that reason, after surveying the situation, he interviewed Mr. Sears and offered him the position temporarily. Following this interview Sears filed his application with the municipal commission.

When it was found that candidate Sears was over age, though he was holding the position under a 12–4 designation, the municipal commission decided to waive the age limit and throw open the examination to all candidates, including non-residents. Following this action, twenty-nine additional applications were received by the municipal commission when the time for filing applications expired on December 30th. Of these twenty-nine additional applicants, Secretary Belcher of the municipal commission testified (p. 6480) that nine were over 50 years of age, and that six were non-residents; a total of ninety-two applications accepted under both advertisements.

President Moskowitz and Secretary Belcher both testified that the applications of candidates under the first advertisement were submitted to Examiner Mayers, who tabulated them and found that but one person had had experience in a "public employment bureau." This person was not Mr. Sears, whose application had been rejected. Both President Moskowitz and Secretary Belcher were asked if such experience was essential to qualify for the position and neither would acknowledge it though both testified that "not enough applicants were qualified to enter an examination," and that for that reason the restrictions against age and residence being removed.

Mr. Sears testified on December 22d that he has acted as temporary superintendent of the Free Employment Bureau since September 16, 1914, having exceeded the time limit of the emergency provision of his appointment by six days, at the time he gave testimony. When the State Commission closed its investigation on January 22, 1915, the written examination for the position of superintendent of the Free Employment Bureau had not been held, and Mr. Sears was then in his position one month and six days *beyond* the period of time allowed under the terms of his appointment — rule 12, paragraphs 3 and 4.

Mr. Sears testified that Commissioner Bell visited him in the Boston office of the Free Employment Bureau of the State of Massachusetts on May 4, 1914, and that he spent the entire day with him.

"Q. (P. 4985) How did he learn of you, did he know you? A. Couldn't help but know of me, I am known all over the country. * * *

"Q. How did you become known? A. Through 20 years and 7 months of *publicity work.* "Q. You were a publicity agent, were you, for the employment bureau? A. I have been a publicity agent prior to accepting my position in Boston."

Mr. Sears testified (p. 4987) that he received $1,800 a year in Boston; that Mr. Bell visited him again in Boston on Labor Day and told him that the salary provided for the position in New York was $3,500 a year, and that Mr. Bell showed him a copy of the city ordinance establishing the free employment bureau. Mr. Sears was asked what method he used for finding employment for unemployed in Boston, and he replied (p. 4988) "we got in touch with employers *through publicity mainly.*"

"Q. (P. 4991) Were you furnishing the employees during the industrial disturbance at Lawrence, the strike-breakers that were used there? A. Surely.

Q. You did? A. Yes, sir. I might explain that lest a bad impression might go out; the office maintained the position of absolute neutrality. We took the order from the employer if there was a strike just as if there was none, always notifying the applicant of all the conditions surrounding it."

The Governor of Massachusetts appointed a committee to investigate the conditions of employment offices in the state. This committee reported on May, 1911, and charged that out of five hundred and five persons reported as having been placed in positions by the Boston free employment bureau of which Mr. Sears had been head for five years, during the month of October, 1910, they ascertained: (4995) "the employers of twenty-four had moved and were not found; letters to two were returned unknown; fifty-eight did not reply to letters; the employers of seventy-six workers replied by letter, and employers of three hundred and forty-five were interviewed. *Of the four hundred and twenty-one employees about whom the Commission obtained information,* 60 *never applied for the position and certainly were never employed, and* 8 *were known to have applied but were not employed. Thus,* 36 *per cent. never entered upon engagement.*"

Mr. Sears was asked if this statement which appears on page 72 of the report of the Massachusetts State Commission was correct. He replied "No" (page 4996). Mr. Sears was also asked why he did not co-operate with the Y. M. C. A. in this city and he replied (page 5006). "Some body from over in Brooklyn called me up, a gentleman, I don't know what his name was, a Mr. Henry or Mr. H. Somebody. It was H. Hawley — he called me on the telephone and said that he wanted to place an engineer, he wanted an engineer and he wanted us to send somebody over to him. I said we could not undertake to do that, as they were a fee agency and it might be implied that we were co-operating on that proposition. I said 'give us the name of the employer and we will do the business direct.'

Q. You didn't co-operate with him in that respect? A. We could not consistently do it.

Q. Are you co-operating with other agencies now? A. No; if the employer will come to us direct, yes.

Q. Are you co-operating with the Atwood agency? A. Yes, we did, because Mrs. Atwood told me that she would waive the fee and that no fee would be charged.

Q. And was not that the case with the Y. M. C. A. Didn't they offer to do the same thing? A. No, sir.

Q. Did you ask them to. A. Yes, sir."

Mrs. Atwood was called as a witness and testified on December 28th (page 5103), that she called up the Free Employment Bureau, some time previously, asked for Mr. Sears and spoke to the person on the telephone telling him that she "wanted some waiters for a shift, and prepared for going out on a voyage, and I gave him the wages and conditions, etc., and I asked him if they can send some men of that character, for we needed a large number and needed them quick." Thirty minutes later she was called up by the same persons with whom she spoke previously who said that they could furnish the help they wanted, and the next morning they sent her two men.

"Q. Did they ask if you would waive the fee? A. No, sir, the waiving of a fee was *not* mentioned and under no conditions.

Q. You made no suggestion to the persons over the telephone that you would waive the fee? A. No, sir, there was no condition and no suggestion made of this kind on either side.

Q. And if Mr. Sears testified — I read from his testimony: 'Are you co-operating with the Atwood Agency? A. Yes, I am, because Mrs. Atwood told me that she is waiving the fee and that no fee would be charged,' is that statement correct? A. *I think not.*

Q. It is not. A. *No,* I have not talked fee to Mr. Sears, I have never talked to him but that once regarding any men and there was no suggestion in regard to any fee at all.

Q. No suggestion made to you about waiving your fees? A. *None whatever.*"

Willis Hawley testified on December 28th that he called up the Free Employment Bureau by telephone and asked for a third class engineer (page 5110). "Well, I said that we had co-operated with the Bureau on Lafayette street in several instances and that we would waive the preliminary fee as we have done, and that we would like to furnish our clients with these men, and that if he had a man on his lists, and if he could send us a man who was investigated and was all right, we would waive the preliminary fee."

Q. (Page 5111) Were you asked by Mr. Sears to waive the fee? A. Why not exactly asked, he stated that he could not co-operate with us if we charged fees.

Q. Did you then offer to waive the preliminary fee? A. I offered then to waive the preliminary fee if the man was investigated and would be guaranteed by him to be all right.

Q. What did he say to that? A. My recollection is that he said, 'well, if anybody happened to come in' he would send him over.

Q. Did he send anyone? A. No.

Q. Did you hear from him after that? A. No."

In view of Mr. Sears' denial of the accuracy of the statements made in the report of the Massachusetts investigating commission, the contradictions of his testimony by Mrs. Atwood and Mr. Hawley must be considered. Mr. Sears' own veracity is in question.

Mr. Sears was asked with reference to the removal of the age restriction in the second advertisement for the position of Superintendent of the Free Employment Bureau (page 5009).

"Q. And didn't you believe the second one was for the purpose of enabling you to enter the examination, you then being in the city's employ temporarily as head of this Bureau? A. Why it was to enable me, with others, *it made it possible for me to take the examination, I don't know whether it was done for my special benefit.*"

Secretary Belcher was asked by President Neu (page 5012):

"Q. Was not Mr. Sears mentioned in the discussion between yourself and the president of the municipal commission and the State Commission at the time the question of raising the age limit, when that was mentioned? Mr. Belcher: *Yes.*

President Neu: And wasn't it said that it was desired to have Mr. Sears admitted to the examination? Mr. Belcher: *It was, I think,* but that is not the statement which you made, Mr. President. The examination was not readvertised for the purpose of admitting Mr. Sears.

President Neu: It was readvertised, wasn't it, for the purpose of admitting Mr. Sears, with others? Mr. Belcher: *Yes, certainly,* the facts of the matter were that we had a dearth of applicants who had the qualifications, even qualifying experience, to say nothing of experience which would count in their favor."

Mr. Sears testified that since he has held the position of Superintendent of the Free Employment Bureau, that he spent money advertising in the daily newspapers for positions and that the corporation counsel informed him that this was in violation of the city charter (page 5014). Since then the expenditure of public money for this purpose stopped.

License Commissioner Bell was asked (page 5137):

"Q. Would not a person who had charge of a great employment bureau, semi-public employment bureau, such as the Y. M. C. A., fit into the position of that kind, and be able to carry that on just as well as a person who had acquired some knowledge from having run a public employment bureau? A. It might be quite possible. I do not think that such a man should be debarred at all from competing for such a position, but the fact is that if I had an opportunity to pick, I would go pick a man that had experience along exactly the lines I needed in the line of running my bureau. * * *

Q. You think a man from out of town coming to the city of New York can operate a bureau of that kind as well as a man with six or seven years' engagement in similar work, although not in a public bureau? A. Well, I think his viewpoint would be better and that he would very speedily get in touch with conditions here.

Q. Wouldn't the other man get in touch with conditions here, knowing the city as he does, and the man who had run a public employment bureau outside of the city, knowing nothing of the city's conditions, wouldn't they be about on an equal basis in getting along? A. Well, one man of course would have an advantage on one side while the other would have an advantage on the other."

Miss Marion White, a clerk in the Free Employment Bureau, testified she was employed as an emergency appointee by Commissioner Bell, that she had worked just one month to December 18th at the rate of $900 per year. Secretary Belcher of the municipal commission acknowledged (page 4896) that a list of temporary clerks, male and female, was in existence. Miss White was *not* taken from the list. She testified on December 21st, that she had worked in the city's employment bureau two days beyond the limit of 30 days specified in paragraph 4 of rule 12 under which she was appointed, but that her services those two days were as a "volunteer." Miss White was still working as a "volunteer" in the Free Employment Bureau the day Commissioner Bell testified, December 28th.

Department of Charities

Charities Commissioner Kingsbury committed an act of gross injustice when he dismissed Samuel Bernstein, for fourteen years a faithful employee of the department, on charges of " inefficiency, neglect of duty and unbusinesslike methods," and the Municipal Civil Service Commission failed in its duty when it permitted the Commissioner to ignore the eligible list when appointing Bernstein's successor.

For twenty years the position of Purchasing Agent in the Charities Department was held by a civil service employee until last December when the Commissioner appointed his former secretary after dismissing Bernstein.

Mr. Bernstein was purchasing agent of the department for a year and two months prior to November 25, 1914, when he was served with charges handed to him by Alfred E. Rejall, private secretary to the Commissioner. He was ordered to defend the charges on the morning of the 27th, the day intervening being Thanksgiving, the order stating " You will be allowed an opportunity of making an explanation in answer thereto before me at the central office of the Department of Public Charities, Municipal Building, Borough of Manhattan, City of New York, at 10:15 in the forenoon on the 27th day of November, 1914, at which time and place you are hereby directed and ordered to be present and prepared to submit your explanation." He was not permitted to have counsel present, and he was found guilty by Commissioner Kingsbury on the testimony of Deputy Commissioners Wright and Thompson, the latter having been in the department only twenty-five days. Mr. Bernstein testified: " Q. (P. 5646) Had Commissioner Kingsbury or Commissioner Thompson or Commissioner Wright ever rebuked you or reproved you for failure to perform your duty as purchasing agent prior to the service of these charges? A. Yes, sir, about the early part of August. I was called into Commissioner Kingsbury's office and the commissioner wanted to know why the people of the City Home were not furnished with clothing and the like. I told him at the time that there were not any funds and when I called the attention of Commissioner Ireland at the time * * * he told me not to issue any orders if the appropriation was exhausted, but to hold on and they could wait a while, and I have written them letters time and time again stating that the appropriations were exhausted, without results. I was not authorized to purchase in the open market and send out orders for that. * * *. Q. You would violate the law if you wrote an order when there was no appropriation? A. I would violate the law if there was not sufficient amount in the appropriation."

Mr. Bernstein testified that the supply accounts for all the institutions under control of the Charities Department were exhausted before August, 1914, and added (p. 5651) "on the 19th of June I wrote a letter to Commissioner Wright, the first deputy, reporting that certain appropriations were exhausted. 'Some of the accounts are very important and a request for transfer should be made at once.' * * *. On June 30th, I wrote another letter: 'Supplementing my letter of the 19th in re: 1914 appropriations overdrawn, would state that it is urgent to have these accounts replenished at the earliest possible moment. Below find list showing the condition of each appropriation for which a transfer is requested and the amount required for the balance of the year.'"

Mr. Bernstein testified that his trial lasted from 10:15 to 12 o'clock on the morning of November 27th, and that he received his notice of dismissal at 4:30 that afternoon. Quoting: "Q. (5667.) Who prosecuted and presented the charges against you? A. Commissioner Kingsbury himself. He brought up all the facts and then asked Commissioner Thompson a few questions and then called in Commissioner Wright. Commissioner Wright was not in at the time and when that second clause there, neglect of duty came up, when I questioned the fact that Commissioner Wright instructed me to follow that out, they called Commissioner Wright in."

Bernstein testified that he explained that whatever he did on which the charges against him were based, was done under orders from one of the Commissioners. He continued (p. 5658): "When Commissioner Kingsbury came in he consolidated both Brooklyn and Richmond and Manhattan and made it under one central purchasing bureau. That was in July, 1914. It meant at least two clerks additional that I ought to receive, and when the matter was brought up to my attention and they asked my opinion on it, I told them it was a very good scheme to consolidate all the purchases, but I would need at least two clerks, a stenographer and a clerk additional. It was promised me at the time by Commissioner Wright, but I never got it."

Bernstein who was an assistant purchasing agent for a year and a half before he took charge of the bureau, was superseded by Alfred E. Rejall, who up to that time had acted as Commissioner Kingsbury's private secretary, *in spite of the fact that an eligible list for purchasing agent of the Charities Department existed.* The position of purchasing agent in the department had been filled from the civil service list for twenty years.

Mr. Rejall testified that he had no experience whatever in the purchase of supplies of any description prior to his appointment to the position. Rejall was acting as purchasing agent thirty days, on a provisional appointment, when questioned by the State Commission.

Mr. Bernstein read in evidence letters to the deputy commissioners dated in May and August, suggesting the transfer of necessary help to the central purchasing bureau, and he testified that as purchasing agent he was responsible for the expenditure of about $450,000 a year, of which about $200,000 was spent on open market orders, the balance going to the State's prisons for material manufactured there. The total expenditure of the department for supplies which he endorsed on contract and open market order was about two and a half million dollars a year (p. 5640).

Mr. Rejall who succeeded Bernstein as purchasing agent, testified that he became secretary to the commissioner in February, 1914, at $2,250 per year; that his salary was increased to $3,000 in April; that he had known the commissioner since he was a student in Columbia University in 1907, and that he was working in the Department of Psychology there prior to his appointment. "Q. (P. 5676.) How is it that you were taken away from your duties as secretary and made acting purchasing agent, how did that come about? A. There was an understanding in February when I was appointed secretary to the Commissioner — * * *. Q. (P. 5677.) Then you understood that you were to give way for the new secretary to the commissioner? A. I won't put it that way sir, by any means. * * *. Q. The Commissioner told you that he intended to appoint a new secretary, didn't he? A. Not that he definitely intended to, that he had in mind the appointment of a certain man providing he might obtain him. * * *. Q. (P. 5678) The agreement was that either you were to make room for this man, for this new secretary, or you were to go out and get another position? A. He would secure me, by a matter of recommendation, provided my services were satisfactory to him, he would secure me some aid in obtaining another position. Q. Mr. Kingsbury kept his word in that respect by giving you this position as acting purchasing agent, he kept his agreement with you in that, is not that so? * * *. Will you answer that question now please, will you say yes or no? A. He appointed me acting purchasing agent; there was no understanding in the beginning that I would be appointed to any position in the department, nothing definite, there was no particular position mentioned by the Commissioner,— no position mentioned, nor was there any mention made that I would receive a particular position, if this other person would come on into the department and serve. Q. You were simply to be taken care of? A. In the sense that anybody, provided I had been satisfactory, would recommend me to anybody else. Q. (P. 5683.) What experience did you have as purchasing agent prior to securing your present position? A. *I said I had never been in a position as purchasing agent.* Q. And when did you first if ever — when, if ever, did you ascertain that Bernstein was not satisfactory as a purchasing agent? A. Why it was I who gave Mr. Bernstein the letter asking him to appear at the hearing; I don't recall the exact date."

How Bernard J. Lally Was Kept Out of a Position in the Charities Department

Bernard J. Lally, who is employed as "hospital helper" on Blackwell's Island, was on the list for deputy lay superintendent at Sea View Hospital on Staten Island. He was notified by Secretary Borden of the Charities Department on February 11, 1914, that his name had been certified for appointment and he replied he would take the place. He received a letter dated March 11th, from Deputy Charities Commissioner Ireland notifying him that his certification from the municipal civil service commission expired *before* Commissioner Kingsbury acted upon it. Lally had "looked over" the place on Staten Island prior to receipt of this communication, at the suggestion of Secretary Borden. On April 3d, he wrote to President Moskowitz of the Municipal Civil Service Commission telling him of what had transpired, that he had *not* been appointed though he signified his willingness to take the place and was the only one on the eligible list who had done so. He received no response from President Moskowitz and a copy of his letter to the president was read in evidence (p. 5837). Lally is still employed as "hospital helper" in the workhouse on Blackwells Island at $480 per year and maintenance. The position at Sea View Hospital pays $600 per year and maintenance. Lally has been in the employ of the city six years; three years with the Charities Department and three years with the Department of Correction. His name was on the eligible list for "hospital clerk" as well as for "deputy lay superintendent of hospitals" and in his letter to President Moskowitz, Lally informs that official, that another person had been appointed "temporarily" to fill the latter position, the title having been changed to "supervisor."

A Medical Director at $6,000 a Year for Thirty Inebriates

Charles Samson, secretary to the inebriety board, an exempt position, testified that he came to this country in 1904, that he became a citizen in 1907, and that he has been in his present position at $3,000 per year since October 1, 1912. He testified that for five years prior to that time he was secretary to Dr. John W. Brannan, President of Bellevue and Allied Hospitals, and that prior to that time he worked under Dr. William H. Allen, former director of the Bureau of Municipal Research, who was general agent of the Association for Improving the Condition of the Poor. The position of secretary to the inebriety board was exempted for his predecessor Dr. William Morrison, but that since Morrison resigned he had occupied the position.

The appropriation for the inebriety board for 1915, is $26,000 and Mr. Samson testified that there were thirty patients in the colony at Warwick, N. Y., where the city owns 800 acres (p.

5814), of whom six were drug victims and the others addicted to drink. The board of inebriety is under the jurisdiction of the Charities Department and Commissioner Kingsbury requested an appropriation of $54,000 for the current year. This was reduced by the board of estimate to the sum allowed. The municipal commission *exempted* Dr. Charles S. Stokes, as medical director of the Board at $6,000 a year and Mr. Samson testified on January 7th, that "we expect to have an average of at least 100 patients throughout the year" (p. 5816).

Commissioner Kingsbury's Friend a "Temporary" Bookkeeper for One Year

Another instance of civil service abuse by Charities Commissioner Kingsbury is the case of Carl Johnson, who was appointed bookkeeper in the Charities Department in January, 1914, at $900 per year.

Johnson knew the Commissioner in Seattle, and was in New York city six months when appointed. He said he asked the Commissioner for a job and that there were vacancies in the bookkeeping staff at the time.

Johnson testified on January 11, 1915 (p. 6240). There had been an examination for bookkeeper toward the end of 1913 and the eligible list was about to be promulgated when the municipal commission went into office January 1, 1914. President Moskowitz explained (p. 6245) that he "cancelled the whole examination and then we gave a new one. Because I cancelled it, naturally it took some time to prepare the new examination, and those who had been acting as 'provisionals' acted still further as 'provisionals,'" *violating the provisions of their appointment.*

Hospital Helpers for All Kinds of Service

This title covers an extensive and systematic violation of law and of civil service principles. The original purpose and reason for these employees was to obtain inexpensive help in city hospitals in menial grades of employment. The salaries are small and the places were occupied by convalescent persons, or those who had nothing better to go to. It has been a matter of comment and conceded by city officials who were witnesses that the grade of ordinary hospital helpers is low, and that they are not ideal attendants upon the sick. Their salaries range from $180 to $480 with maintenance and occasionally run to $600 or $720 without maintenance. The custom of using the more intelligent and reliable of these persons for clerical services had a natural origin in the hospital, but the custom has been pushed to such an extreme that it amounts now *to a gross violation of law.*

"Hospital Helpers" Working in Many Capacities in Departments of Charities, Health and Bellevue and Allied Hospitals

The title is frequently used to circumvent the law, and in many instances it affects seriously the rights of persons on eligible lists and the rights of laboring men, because in some of the hospitals, hospital helpers are working as *mechanics* alongside of real mechanics, and their payrolls passed on false certifications. The evil has gone so far that in some instances where a commissioner desires to employ a friend and has no appropriation or other position available, he appoints the individual as a "hospital helper" (though he never visits a hospital) and is employed as clerk or stenographer or something similar in spite of the fact that he is certified as "hospital helper." In the ordinary situation the Municipal Civil Service Commission does not know that the payroll certificate is false, but in many instances the facts were shown publicly to the municipal commission in our hearings; but the violations continued.

Mr. Spencer, former secretary of the local civil service commission testified (page 444) that about two years previous an agreement was reached between the hospital authorities and the civil service commission then in office that hospital helpers who were performing clerical work in hospitals and in the offices of the heads of the departments of Charities, Health and Bellevue and Allied hospitals should be classed as "hospital clerks." If they received more than $480 a year they would fall into the competitive class — indicated by an eligible list. Notwithstanding this agreement the "hospital helper" is a worse evil to-day than ever before, and this is largely due to the attitude of the Charities Commission which has not been effectively checked by the Municipal Civil Service

Commission. *The Municipal Commission surrendered in the matter of the forty-seven examiners and it has surrendered in nearly every other instance, thereby becoming party to the wrong.*

On October 21, 1914, Florence Rowland was called as a witness (page 212). She had been employed in the central office of the Department of Charities in the Municipal Building since June 22, 1914, as stenographer and typewriter. She was paid as "hospital helper." Miss Lohman (confidential secretary to Commissioner Kingsbury) tested her as a stenographer and she was employed at $50 a month, and worked there steadily until she appeared before us as a witness, September 29th; she signed the application for employment as "hospital helper" was carried on the payroll as "hospital helper" and was so certified.

Clyde B. Rose was examined (p. 218). He had known Commissioner Kingsbury in Seattle. He came from Seattle to take part in the boat races at Poughkeepsie. He was in New York city one week when he was employed by Commissioner Kingsbury. He opened the Commissioner's mail and classified it for reading, worked on his tickler system and executed special assignments as an investigator, examining requisitions and the like. He had no notion of doing hospital work and said if it were required of him he would resign. He thought himself too good for menial work, he said though he was willing to start in the Commissioner's office at $50 a month. *But,* he had to sign an application for appointment as "hospital helper," was appointed as such, was put on the payroll, certified and paid as such. Secretary Borden (p. 225) who as one of the Board of Examiners of the Charities Department had certified that he was free from physical disease, was morally competent, etc., had given him no examination whatever. It developed that those certificates are habitually so made out by said local board, and are false, because there is no such examination as certified. (See Wright, p. 225; Ireland, p. 270.) The form so certified states that the board has examined the candidate and finds that he or she is free from physical disease or defect which is likely to interfere with the discharge of duties; that general character is satisfactory; that candidate possesses the requisite knowledge, ability and experience, and that "*such person is appointed to perform the duties appropriate to their titles and are not to be assigned to perform duties appertaining to another title.*" It is signed by Henry C. Wright and Gordon Ireland, Commissioners, and J. McKee Borden, Secretary, acting as a board of examiners for non-competitive classes. *It was absolutely and knowingly false.*

The same form of certificate was made for Miss Rowland, and for all the persons who were set to clerical, stenographic and similar work. As no physical examinations are given by this board the certification is *false* as to the mass of real hospital helpers appointed from time to time, and this fact is important in view of the well founded statements and testimony that the ranks of the real hospital helpers are infested with "rounders and habitual drunkards." These two unfortunate persons, Miss Rowland and Mr. Rose, had upset things with their unexpected testimony, and all hands ran to cover. On October 8th, the municipal commission notified Commissioner Kingsbury that Mr. Rose and Miss Rowland were doing work "*manifestly in violation of the Civil Service Law,*" that their payrolls would not be passed and that they had informed the Comptroller of their action under section 20 of the Civil Service Law. The notification concluded with these words: "Assignments of hospital helpers *similar to the assignments of Mr. Rose and Miss Rowland will be treated in the same manner by this commission.*"

But again the civil service commission surrendered to the charities commissioner, and though many of these cases were revealed and their payrolls exhibited, the commissioner never acted again. These two poor, young witnesses, and Miss Wallace, next mentioned, completed the sacrifice. If our commission had accepted the brave promise of the local body and let it go at that, the system of violations would have gone on undiscovered and unchecked. The cases of Miss Rowland and Mr. Rose were supposed at the time to be exceptional and we treated them only incidentally (p. 293), but being informed that Miss Anna Wallace was engaged in the commissioner's office in the same way and capacity as Miss Rowland, a process server was sent to subpoena her. The commissioner personally interfered, created a diversion by a closed door, Miss Wallace got away without being served, left her position, and never afterwards could be secured as a witness. (See pp.

155, 165, 167, 169.) It appeared that Miss Wallace was one of the special forty-seven charity examiners appointed by Commissioner Kingsbury as previously shown. Being dropped from that position on September 1st she was assigned to do stenographic work for Deputy Commissioner Wright and was appointed as a hospital helper.

(NOTE.— Commissioner Wright was assisting the process server to find Miss Wallace who was in the office when Mr. Kingsbury or someone else in his presence interfered.)

On January 11, 1915, when the investigation was nearly ended, the main office of the commissioner of charities in the Municipal building was again called upon, and we saw how futile was the lesson of October, 1914, and the sacrifice of Rose, Rowland and Wallace, and the brave letter of the Municipal Civil Service Commission.

(1) Cletus R. Conway, rated, certified and paid as a "hospital helper," was found to be the stenographer and copyist for the purchasing agent at $720 a year, and entirely innocent of hospitals. She had been working previously under the title of "clerical assistant," why her title was changed she didn't know but she continued to do the same work (p. 6207).

(2) Helen Ryan, rated, certified and paid as a "hospital helper," was found to be serving the same person in the same capacity as Miss Conway, at $720 (p. 6209).

(3) Anna McCann, rated, certified and paid as "hospital helper," was found to be acting as stenographer to the chief engineer, Mr. Herrick, at $720. This lady is on the civil service eligible list for typewriter copyist, but never accepted a position, receiving more money as "hospital helper." She never visited a hospital (p. 6212).

(4) Marian G. Regan, is rated, certified and paid as a "hospital helper," is the stenographer and typewriter for Mr. Borden, secretary of the department, at $600 (p. 6214).

(5) Carrile R. Weaver is rated, certified and paid as "hospital helper" but is actually general clerk and stenographer to Mr. Dunwoodie, one of the general inspectors in the department, at $600 (p. 6217). She was an "emergency stenographer" in

Brooklyn, was dropped, and then came to New York as "hospital helper."

In these cases consider the intentional false certifying: First the application of the candidate is falsely certified, then the payroll is falsely certified. That payroll goes to the Municipal Civil Service Commission and is again certified. If the commission doesn't know the facts it ought to. *What is the result?* The comptroller pays out the salary warrants on the strength of those false certificates, but if he knew the facts as he did in the cases of Miss Rowland and Mr. Rose he would refuse payment on all of them. It is not within our function to discuss the question of *criminality*.

At the same hearing instances of the same evil were shown in the same department, in other offices than in the Municipal building.

(1) Julia C. Clark, hospital helper, has charge of the application book and interviews and enrolls patients at the tuberculosis hospital (p. 6246).

(2) Ida M. Robins, chief of the forty-seven charity examiners, whose work is entirely in the office in Schermerhorn street, Brooklyn, is rated, certified and paid as a "nurse" *for September, October and November,* 1914, *after she was dropped as "charity examiner," though she continued to do the same work. This false certification was permitted by the Municipal Commission, her change of title from "charity examiner" to "nurse" having been disclosed in her testimony in October and previously.*

(3) Matilda G. Reamer was another of the forty-seven dropped for some reason. She continued to act as application clerk at the Schermerhorn street office, but she was rated, certified and paid as "hospital helper" (p. 6847).

As to Mrs. Reamer, Commission Kingsbury said: Her "payroll title is hospital helper, and the office title is application clerk, and there was a vacancy in the positions of application clerk and hospital helper and she was appointed to the place by (deputy) Commissioner Doherty" (p. 6891).

A list of "hospital helpers" furnished by the commissioner of charities early in the investigation (October 14, 1914) by direction of the State Commission, showed 135 "hospital helpers" who were doing work *inappropriate* to their titles. The commissioner certified that they worked as stenographers, typewriters, clerks, employment agents, reception agents, index clerks, milk inspectors, messengers, application clerks, audit clerks, file clerks, registers, attendants, caretakers, matrons, telephone operators, storekeepers, storehouse and ledger clerks, file clerks, bookkeepers, information clerks, payroll clerks, chief clerks. Twenty-one of these were in his own office in the Municipal building as employment agents, stenographers, and typewriters, reception agents, clerks, milk inspectors, etc. A similar condition, he stated, existed in the central office in Brooklyn (p. 744 to 758.)

This report was produced before the representatives of the Municipal Commission and was summarized in their hearing.

At one of our last sessions President Moskowitz was asked whether his commission had stopped the payrolls of any other "hospital helpers" beside that of Mr. Rose and Miss Rowland and he replied that he had *not*.

The International Brotherhood of Stationary Firemen (p. 738) protested against the employment of Henry Hassenbeck, Thomas O'Connell and Charles Weaver, "hospital helpers," as boiler firemen and oilers in the Metropolitan Hospital. They were being paid $120 a year and were doing the same work for which regular workmen in same place were receiving $3 a day. The protest was made to the Municipal Commission several times without result (p. 740). The grades of oilers and boiler firemen are classified (p. 7421). Hospital helpers are noncompetitive.

A report from Bellevue and Allied Hospitals shows 181 persons listed as "hospital helpers" at salaries ranging from $300 to $480, 4 at $600, and 1 at $720, working as telephone operators, clerks, stenographers, typewriters, property clerks, copyists, pharmacists, chemists, assistants in X-ray laboratory, gatemen, foremen, laborers, etc., assistants in shops, elevator runners, storekeepers, registrars, laboratory assistants, morgue keepers, storekeepers, and carpenters (p. 2251).

Municipal Lodging-house Run by Provisional Appointee Whiting and a "Hospital Helper"

William A. Whiting had conducted an investigation into the affairs of a lodging-house for the charities commissioner and on this report charges were made against the incumbent who was suspended on April 26th, at which time Whiting succeeded him as *temporary* superintendent. On June 10th Whiting was appointed under Rule 12, paragraph 4, to fill an *emergency.* On July 29 he was given a noncompetitive examination to qualify for provisional appointment under Rule 12, paragraph 3, and was holding that position under such appointment on the day he testified (October 23), *no competitive examination having been held up to that time. Whiting exceeded the time limit of his Rule* 12, *paragraph* 4 *appointment by eighteen days and he was in the position as provisional appointee* a month beyond the time allowed in Rule 12, paragraph 3 at the time he testified. His payroll was passed under special certification by the Municipal Commission pending the outcome of the noncompetitive examination and there was no prospect at the time he testified that a competitive examination for the position would be held by the end of the year.

Mr. Whiting was asked if he hoped to get the position of superintendent in the event of the dismissal of the man he was investigating and he replied, "I expected to get it, yes" (p. 1223). He said he wanted the job because "of the opportunity it gave for social service" (p. 1224), and he acknowledged that he spoke about it to Commissioner Kingsbury before he was appointed on April 26th. He said the commissioner asked him with reference to his general qualifications and experience *before* he undertook the investigation of the administration of the lodging-house (p. 1225). "Q. And thereafter you were appointed to investigate? A. Yes."

Whiting's noncompetitive examination was conducted in violation of Rule 7, paragraph 9, which specifies that "all examinations shall be in *writing* except such as relate to physical qualities and except as herein otherwise provided." The provision requires that a stenographic record of oral questions and answers be filed. President Moskowitz of the Municipal Commission testified that there was *no* stenographic record of the noncompetitive examination given to Whiting and Whiting testified that the only "examination" he was subjected to was when an investigator named Simpson called at the lodging-house and asked him questions about the duties of the position.

Whiting was assisted in his investigation by a man named Sigmund Simon whom he "picked up" at the lodging-house, and who acted as "assistant superintendent" (pp. 1350 and 1351). Simon is recorded on the payroll of the charities department as a "hospital helper" at a salary of $720 a year. He first received $480 a year, which was increased, he said, September 1. Simon testified that he first met Whiting in March and that he assisted from that time until he was appointed "hospital helper." In that capacity Simon acted as the "strong-arm" of the institution. He said that he was subjected to no examination other than questions put to him by Whiting, and that Mr. Whiting "talked casually about different affairs connected with the lodging-house" (p. 1353). Mr. Whiting was one of the persons to whom Simon referred as a "character reference" on April 22, when he filled out a statement which is filed with the Civil Service Commission and Whiting signed the statement as a witness. That statement and the references were never verified by them. Recently, as stated above, Simon disappeared from the lodging-house with $180 belonging to a lodger. Third Deputy Commissioner Thompson testified that he investigated the charge of Walter J. Sloane, former steward, that he was beaten at the lodging-house by Simon in the presence of Whiting, and he recommended Simon's *dismissal* for conduct unbecoming an employee of the city. This recommendation was made three weeks before Simon disappeared and it was not acted upon by Commissioner Kingsbury. That commissioner kept Simon in his place as assistant superintendent after he had been notified publicly that it was illegal to allow him to do such work under the title of hospital helper. In Commissioner Kingsbury's violation of law the Municipal Civil Service Commission participated with full knowledge, certifying and passing him on the payrolls. It appears that many of the inmates of the lodging-house have money and that special arrangements are made to care for it.

The Forty-seven Examiners of Charitable Institutions

For many years the Department of Charities has maintained a force of "Examiners of Charitable Institutions" whose duties included the re-examination of cases in which children had been committed as defectives and otherwise, to Randall's Island and to the various child caring institutions. These employees operated mainly through three bureaus controlled by Superintendents Thorne, Bauer and Dodworth. Children supposed *and known* to be mentally defective have been referred by the various courts and societies to a bureau organized by an eminent specialist, Dr. Schlapp, through whose clearing house for mental defectives, their status and condition were determined, and if proper they have been sent to the hospital for children on Randall's Island. These superintendents are men of experience, tact and ability and the work of re-investigation has been very faithfully performed with the force of examiners at their disposal. While there has been no social service program (as understood in certain lately developed circles) there has been a plain and practical social work done by these investigators as far as they have been able to do it, incidental to their work. There has been sensible and practical co-operation between the examiners and the various private charities of the city so that the cases of need and distress have been referred to these societies for their very effective treatment.

Recently Dr. Edward T. Devine has accepted a temporary appointment in the Department of Charities for the purposes among others, of developing a more definite social service program in connection with the work of the examiners whose numbers have been enlarged, and he testified that he has found excellent material among the old examiners, and that in his grouping of the examiners, his instructing them and his urging for the new, social service program, he is receiving encouraging assistance from a large proportion of these old examiners.

Early in 1914, it appears that the Commissioner of the Department of Charities began to proceed with a program for enlarging his force of examiners. There was an eligible list in existence from which appointments easily could be made upon the transfer of funds to the Charities Department to provide for their salaries. This eligible list contained many persons of good practical experience,— people who had lived in the City of New York for a long time and who were familiar with practical problems of life in crowded parts of the city. Many of these have done volunteer work for years in the charitable societies connected with churches and synagogues. But it was not part of the commissioner's program or desire to accept candidates from that list. He desired to make personal selections and personal appointments and he and his advisers turned to rule 12 for help. Paragraph 6 of that rule provided that:

> "The Commission may by resolution except from competitive examination any person engaged in *private* business who shall render any professional, scientific, technical or expert service of an occasional and exceptional character to any city officer and the amount of whose compensation in any one year shall not exceed $750."

It was designed in appointing under this clause, if the local civil service commission would permit it, to have the employments run for six months at the rate of $1,200 a year (which would be within the $750 provision), and in the meanwhile to procure another eligible list to follow the old list on its expiration near the end of the year. The first problem was to secure a transfer of funds to pay the salaries. A long and careful statement was made to the comptroller who, in turn, presented it to the board of estimate and apportionment and on that statement $42,750 was transferred from the food and supplies account (used by hospitals, etc.) of the Department of Charities to pay the salaries. In the comptroller's report it was stated that this proceeding was most unusual and would be subject to criticism unless there was a very good reason for it and that reason was stated to be the claim by the commissioner of charities that if his force of examiners were enlarged so that adequate re-examinations could be made, the additional re-examinations would result in the removal from child caring institutions of so many dependents that the cutting out of the allowances made for the care of those children would result in a *saving to the city* of many times the salaries, and at the same time discourage those who suffered their children to be placed as charges upon the treasury of the city. *There was no word expressed in the report of the commissioner upon which the comptroller's report was based nor in the comptroller's report, expressive of any intention to organize a social service program with the new examiners.* No doubt there were men in the board of estimate and apportionment who understood that that project was included in the proposition, but it is just as certain that there were other men in the board of estimate and apportionment who were *not informed of this relatively expensive program, nor of the new social service scheme that was to be built up, by a transfer of food supply funds.*

The money being appropriated, the next step was to evade the eligible list upon which many worthy people had been long waiting for appointments. When the commissioner of charities addressed the Municipal Civil Service Commission asking that his appointees be excepted, it did except them upon a proposition not mentioned to the board of estimate and apportionment, namely, that it was intended to do a new work of social service — of the rehabilitation of families which would require just the kind of people as examiners who are described in paragraph 6 of rule 12. It appears that the persons whom the commissioner had selected to appoint were already known and designated when the resolution was adopted. That resolution was not put through the Municipal Civil Service Commission without discussion and division of opinion and it seems clear that the resolution was passed without the concurrence of one of the commissioners who held that the proposal was *not lawful.*

The State Civil Service Commission examined a large proportion of the forty-seven persons who were appointed to these important positions without competitive examination, and who by their temporary service gained practical advantages which helped them materially to get upon the new eligible list which recently was made up to supersede the old eligible list. Conceding that several of the forty-seven were persons of good qualifications and experience, it was perfectly plain that in general these new examiners did *not* meet the requirements of section 6, which was tortured to permit their appointment. The report of the commissioner of charities upon which the financial provision for the forty-seven was made by the board of estimate, contained a careful computation of the number of cases that must be re-investigated, in the time (six months) in which it must be done, of the average number of cases per day that an investigator could handle, with the final straight result that it required just that number of examiners to re-investigate that number of cases. The computing was so carefully done as to run into decimals. It was conceded by the commissioner and his subordinates that rehabilitation work requires very much more time than investigating and that the average number of cases that can be handled for social service is very much *fewer* than those which can be handled for reinvestigating. *Our investigation showed clearly that if the forty-seven were to be used for the purposes expressed to the board of estimate and apportionment they could not do social service or rehabilitation work, and also that if they were to be used for social service and rehabilitation they could not accomplish the reinvestigation which was urged as the basis for the financial provision.*

The persons who were appointed were relatively young and lacking in the experiences of life. Relatively they had more college and special training than the old examiners or eligibles but that was discounted by their lack of experience in the world and in the real problems of life. *Two of the persons appointed were under twenty-one years of age and two of them were not citizens.* Some had to be dropped soon, because they did not qualify in the service. They had come largely from the employment bureau associated with the School of Philanthropy where they registered and paid a fee. One of those dropped had been recommended by President Moskowitz of the municipal commission. He rendered false reports. It might be supposed that to qualify forty-seven appointments upon the ground of "peculiar and exceptional qualifications of a scientific, professional or educational character," that there would have been a careful examination made and recorded of each one of the appointees. The fact as developed in the testimony given before us, and the admissions of the commissioner and his assistants, was that the *examinations were short and perfunctory, lasting in some cases five minutes and occasionally twenty minutes, that no record was kept of those examinations, that nothing could be shown to indicate what the inquiries and answers were and that in some cases the selection proceeded upon the ground of personal acquaintance and recommendation.*

Several of the persons upon the eligible list were examined by us in order to get a view of their personalities. Some of the old examiners were questioned and it was found that without special instructions they had been doing some social work (until the forty-seven were appointed), that there was relatively as much humanitarianism among the old examiners and the persons on the eligible list as could be found in the forty-seven, with as much probability of responsiveness to a definite program of organization and instruction upon the *new notion* of social service in the Charities Department. As the claim for the exception of the forty-seven was based upon a claim of very special and extraordinary qualification, quite a number of cases were examined in which the new temporary examiners had worked and wherein it was found that their conduct was distinguished by a *failure to appreciate and act upon the principles of humanity.* It was found that ordinarily the new examiners had proceeded with the main proposition in view of accomplishing a *reduction of the city's expenses* by removing dependents from the children's hospital and from child caring institutions, and that their primary purpose was *not the relieving and helping of persons afflicted with poverty and sickness. "Social service" was forgotten.* There were some instances shown where the new examiners had done helpful work while investigating, but it was no greater in degree and quality than that which appears to have been done regularly by the good old-fashioned examiners, moved by humane impulses which attend them while they are upon their duties.

It was not with any intention of overhauling the general conduct of the Department of Charities that these cases were examined, but entirely for the purpose of observing in action the new force of examiners excepted from competitive examination, upon the ground of *peculiar* qualities and qualifications and likely to be permanently grafted upon the city's civil service list through the competitive examination which they were to take, with the advantage of several months' experience in the positions temporarily held and with the specialized training and acquired terminology of charity experts who organized the new movement.

A summation of the whole matter is this: A complete reinvestigation to determine whether there were unworthy cases in the children's hospital and in the child-caring institutions required exactly the old force of investigators, plus the forty-seven who were provided for in the action of the board of estimate on purely *economical grounds — and on no program of social service, and who might just as well have been taken from the standing eligible list.* They could have done the social work on the side as they have been doing by the use of kind words and helpful suggestions and by referring cases of need and distress to the A. I. C. P. the dispensaries and other charitable institutions. The ignoring of the eligible list and going to the Municipal Civil Service Commission for an exception under Rule 12 paragraph 6 *was simply a device to beat the list and did not result in securing* " experts " such as are described in the rule. It did not open a real program of social service any different from that which was carried on by the old examiners and which is being followed and enlarged by Doctor Devine with the effective help of the old examiners, for carrying the humane spirit into their work. The augmented force is no greater than necessary to do thorough re-investigating of dependent cases with humanity and helpfulness on the side.

The temporary excepted examiners were not specially humane, and their conduct in many cases shown in our subjoined Table D, shows that *some of them were heartless and were more intent on putting children out of places and thereby saving money for the city, than they were of helping the poor and the distressed.*

To do a real inspirational social work among the poor properly and effectively, would require a much larger force than has been provided for or contemplated, and would impinge on the excellent work of private organizations that are all within reach by an enlargement of the policy of coordination between the examiners and the societies that has long existed.

The view of the Board of Estimate is shown in the fact that the salaries for the new social service investigators coming from the new list that has been established have been fixed at $900 to $1,050 and $1,200 (instead of all at $1,200).

James P. Conway (1419, etc.), who was formerly Assistant Chief Examiner of the Municipal Civil Service Commission, took part in preparing and rating the examination for the former eligible list. He had considerable experience in social service

(p. 1550). He made a comparison of the papers of 40 of those candidates, with the statements of 35 of the 47 made to the State Civil Service Commission, as to their experience and qualifications. He said (p. 1425) *that those on the eligible list were in general well qualified by age, experience and fundamental education, and some were exceptionally well qualified.* Out of 40 examined, 30 were between 26 and 40 years of age, and only 2 were under 26. As for the new appointees, they had good fundamental schooling, *but lacked in training* after leaving school and in business matters, *and were particularly lacking in investigation experience.* Of the 35 examined, 10 were *under* 26 years of age, and 19 were under 35. Twelve of these had not been employed since leaving school, or their occupations were meagre. On the whole, the qualifications of those on the old eligible list for practical work, *were superior.* That opinion is *sustained on all the evidence in the case.*

The Commissioner of Charities on August 6, 1914, wrote to the Municipal Commission and said:

> "The persons whom we desire to enlist in the work are real experts within the meaning of Rule 12, Clause 6. The service which they are to render is distinctly, 'expert service of an occasional or exceptional character.'"

On July 25 he had notified that commission that the appointment of the 47 had been made, and referred to July 7 as the date of an agreement for their appointment. On that letter one of the clerks of the commission endorsed a reference to the *existing eligible list,* and did the same on a similar letter dated August 6, 1914.

John A. Daly, one of the old regular force of examiners testified (p. 4726) that he protested directly to President Moskowitz against the appointment of the 47 as an injury to those who had entered the department in the regular way. He said (p. 4730) there was dissention, antagonism and disorganization of the employees by the reflection upon them (that they were not fitted for the kind of work to be done); that the examiners felt they were not getting a square deal. At a conference of the examiners attended by Commissioner Kingsbury, he declared that the social service idea was nothing new, and that the old examiners had been working on those lines. He said: *That since that time he had not been invited to conferences, and he has been transferred to Staten Island and has the whole of that island to cover alone.*

Conclusion

In concluding our report, we regret to have to say that the Municipal Civil Service Commission has shown itself in many respects to be weak and inefficient. The integrity of the law lies with the local commission. In some cases the Commission has neglected its duty; in others it has not seen its duty; in others it has concurred in evasions and violations; and it has violated the law itself. The dominating member has been the President, and on him rests the greatest share of the blame. He has demonstrated himself to be temperamentally incompetent and impractical, while the other members failed to grasp opportunities to offset these defects and resultants thereof.

The Commission expresses its high appreciation of the services of Special Deputy Attorney-General, Frank Moss, and of Henry H. Klein, whom it employed as investigator.

JACOB D. NEU, President.
MEYER WOLFF, M. D.,
JAMES A. LAVERY,
State Civil Service Commissioners.

TABLE "A"

Cases in Physical Examinations

Note. When Mr. Curtis was examined and showed an absence of physical tests except dumb bell and eye chart test in the examination for salary and grade examiner, President Moskowitz said (1012) that if it was true, the examination was not up to the standard; that the notice specifying many requirements that were not really exacted on the examination, was not right. He said,

" I am very grateful because I am going to find out why the man didn't get the examination indicated on the card " (1017). He said he didn't see why there should be a difference between that examination and the finger-print examination. He said, " We want physically sound bodies in the city's service " (1023). Mr. Coudert intervened and said, " He says this now, that *as soon as you point out anything bad, he will try to carry it out.*" (Mr. Coudert's language was unusually ambiguous, but no doubt he meant, well.)

President Neu responded: " That is what we are here for " and Mr. Coudert answered, " That is what we are all here for."

But the proofs as we went along showed that the promise of the early report was not kept, and that in most of the examinations, despite the advertisements, there were no physical tests except the *old ones of dumb-bell and eye chart, and that those often were administered and marked unfairly and wrong.*

Cases. Michael J. Gannon (905), Claude F. Curtis (914), Fred W. Taylor (1083), Leo Reich (2013), Mrs. B. Irvine (2411), Miles S. Vickery (2815), James A. Burns (2903), Walter F. Tracy (2906), Wm. E. Schuster (2910), Rose Webber (2912), J. C. Lyons (2914), Benjamin Schwartz (2917), Flora Biddlecomb (2818), Adrian D. Stevenson (2880, 2873), Lillian Wolf (2880), Carroll Klein (2897), Sidney W. Reeves (3090, 2848), Nathan Applebaum (3076), Frank H. Hinnin (3079), Edw. F. Cooney (3096), David Scott (3112), Victor J. Matthews (3124), Thomas A. Kennedy (3127), Bertha Herbig (3224), Theresa Heslau (3227), Barbara Brown (3228), Catharine Northrop (3231), Thos. Dunworth (2393), Isaac Levy (3246), Catharine A. Washkey (3249), Anna K. Solan (4907), Esther Polinsky (4914), Mary A. Greenberg (4916), Geo. P. Burke (4921), John O'Connor (4923), Francis M. O'Keefe (4931), Nina Prey (4935), Leopold A. Greco (5084).

See statement of strict physical examination for *elimination* purposes where there are many candidates (2894).

See the sending out of invitations for re-examination after rejection, *without* requests from candidates, when the State Commission was " poking into " the physical examination books (2880–1).

TABLE "B"

Cases in Policemen's Physical Examinations

Our examinations included only a few of the cases that appeared in the books, and we show the results of our inquiries into them.

Policemen rejected on minimum height of 5 ft. 7 2/5 in. (1/10 of an inch short); Fred Borho (3104); D. R. Breen (3106); Arthur Lassen (3106); Louis F. DeMars (3342); B. Marchesi (3347); Francis M. Morton (3349); John S. Haugh (3351).

The above is noted because Mr. Ruddy's testimony quoted in the main part of the testimony shows how careless he has been; how candidates might stand as they pleased so long as their feet touched the floor; how bumps, etc. were allowed. In some of the cases above noted *subsequent measurements showed the men tall enough.*

(3046, 3051, 3116, 3070, 3104, 3217, 3305, 3422. Dr. Warbasse and Mr. Ruddy. 3353 Mr. Murray as to interrupted effort to improve the system.)

Jacob Katz (3145, 3161)

December, 1913, 5 ft. 7¼ in., rejected. March, 1914, 5 ft. 7½ in., passed. November 18, 1914, 5 ft. $7\frac{7}{10}$ in.

In this and following cases, the last measurement given was made for the State Commission at one of its hearings, *the candidate standing under the same measuring rod with bare feet.*

Edward F. Devine (3151)

January, 1914, 5 ft. 7¼ in., rejected. March, 1914, 5 ft. 7½ in., passed. November, 1914, 5 ft. 7½ in.

This candidate had discharge papers of the U. S. A. and had been measured at 5 ft. 7½ inches; why was he rejected in January, 1914?

Daniel W. Chrystie (3178)

January 9, 1914, 5 ft. 9¾ in. March 6, 1914, 5 ft. 9½ in. This candidate was rejected in January for flat foot, bought an arch in a shoe store and in March the doctor passed him. He declared he was 5 ft. 10 in.

Thomas A. Mulholland (3162)

December, 1913, 5 ft. 7½ in., 136 pounds. March, 1914, 5 ft. 7¾ in., 140 pounds. November, 1914, 5 ft. 8¼ in. He was first rejected because less than 140 pounds, but had weighed at Church House gymnasium at 141 pounds, the night before and the night after at 141½ pounds.

Harold Steinhardt (3167)

December, 1913, 5 ft. 7 2/5 in., 137½ pounds. March, 1914, 5 ft. 7½ in., 141 pounds. November, 1914, 5 ft. 7 6/10 in.

This candidate had been measured by Dr. Messenger (a well known physician) at 5 ft. 7⅝ in. and 140 pounds, and later at the 69th Regiment at 5 ft. 7¾ inches and 142 pounds.

Louis Oliver (3173)

December, 1913, 5 ft. 7½ in., 136 pounds, rejected. March, 1914, 5 ft. 8 in., 140 pounds, passed. November, 1914, 5 ft. 7 9/10 in., 136 pounds, *dressed.*

Felix McKenna (3186)

January, 1914, 5 ft. 10 in., 144 pounds, rejected, light. March, 1914, 5 ft. 9½ in., 146½ pounds, passed. November, 1914, 5 ft. 9 in., 147½ pounds, *dressed.*

On re-examination, March, 1914, this man's height was reduced, and his weight was increased, so he passed.

Frederick Reichardt (3193)

December, 1913, 6 ft. 3½ in., 171 pounds, rejected, light. March, 1914, 6 ft. 2½ in., 175 pounds, passed. November, 1914, 6 ft. 1½ in.

This candidate was measured shorter in March and weighed heavier, so he passed; at the State Commission's hearing he was measured even *shorter.* On the same scales, in the same year, measured by an athletic expert, he varied two inches. His rejection in December included defective vision as a reason, but in March defective vision was not discovered.

Thomas F. Byrnes (3201)

December, 1913, 5 ft. 7½ in., 138 pounds, rejected. March, 1914, 5 ft. 7½ in., 140 pounds, passed. November, 1914, 5 ft. 7 6/10 in., 139½ pounds *dressed*.

F. A. Ulschmid (3210)

January, 1914, 5 ft. 7½ in., 139½ pounds. November, 1914, 5 ft. 7 6/10 in.

This candidate was rejected for one-half pound light weight and didn't know enough to ask for re-examination in March.

William A. La Tour, Jr. (3310)

December, 1913, 5 ft. 7½ in. November, 1914, 5 ft. 8¼ in.

A. J. Finamore (3314)

March, 1914, 5 ft. 7½ in. (in re-examination). November, 1914, 5 ft. 7 9/10 in.

John J. Hoffman (3317)

December, 1913, 5 ft. 7½ in., 139 pounds, rejected. March, 1914, 5 ft. 8 in., 143 pounds, passed. November, 1914, 5 ft. 7 9/10 in., 142 pounds, *dressed*.

F. Rodenwald (3320)

March 2, 1914, 5 ft. 7½ in., 140 lbs., re-examined and passed. November, 1914, 5 ft. 7¾ in., 143 pounds, *dressed*.

William J. Cronin (3322)

December, 1913, 5 ft. 7½ in., 140 pounds. November, 1914, 5 ft. 7½ in. plus 1/10, 140¾ pounds *dressed*.

This candidate passed in December, 1913, as to the exact minimum of height and weight.

William J. McCormick (3324)

December, 1913, 5 ft. 7½ in. November, 1914, 5 ft. 7¾ in.

L. B. Jozwink (3325)

December, 1913, 5 ft. 7½ in. November, 1914, 5 ft. 7¾ in.

J. J. Gunson (3326)

January, 1914, 5 ft. 7½ in. November, 1914, 5 ft. 7 2/5 in. In December this candidate was just squeezed in.

W. L. Moran (3328)

January, 1914, 5 ft. 7½ in. November, 1914, 5 ft. 7¾ in.

Jos. Rudolph (3329)

December, 1913, 5 ft. 7½ in., 139½ lbs., rejected. March, 1914, 5 ft. 7¾ in., 140½ lbs. November, 1914, 5 ft. 7½ in., 136 lbs., *dressed.*

In December, 1913, this candidate was rejected for lack of ½ pound, but in March he had *gained* a pound. In November he was woefully *below* weight, according to Ruddy's measurements.

Martin J. Palmer (3331)

January, 1914, 5 ft. 7½ in. November, 1914, 5 ft. 7¾ in.

John F. Murray (3333)

December, 1913, 5 ft. 7½ in. November, 1914, 5 ft. 7¾ in.

Jas. J. Kiernan (3335)

December, 1913, 5 ft. 7½ in. November, 1914, 5 ft. 7¾ in.

A. O. Kreiss (3336)

December, 1913, 5 ft. 7½ in. November, 1914, 5 ft. 7 3/5 in.

L. F. De Mars (3342)

March, 1914, 5 ft. 7 2/5 in., rejected on re-examination. November, 1914, 5 ft. 7 4/5 in.

The measurement made for the State Commission by Ruddy, if made in March, would have *passed* the candidate.

Fred Borho (3344)

The same measurement and comment as for De Mars.

John S. Haigh (3351)

The same measurement and comment as for De Mars.

B. Marchesi (3347)

December, 1913, 5 ft. 7 2/5 in., rejected. March, 1914, 5 ft. 7 2/5 in., rejected. November, 1914, 5 ft. 7½ in.

Same comment as above.

Francis D. Morrow (3349)

March, 1914, 5 ft. 7 2/5 in. November, 1914, 5 ft. 7¼ in.

Jos. F. Walker (3350)

December, 1913, 5 ft. 7¼ in. November, 1914, 5 ft. 7 in.

H. E. Kennedy (3411)

December, 1914, 5 ft. 7½ in. March, 1913, 5 ft. 7½ in. November, 1914, 5 ft. 7 9/10 in.

This candidate was rejected in December for defective vision, but passed in March.

H. F. Scherenbrand (3413)

December, 1913, 5 ft. 7½ in. November, 1914, 5 ft. 7 3/5 in.

John J. Donnelly (3414)

December, 1913, 5 ft. 7¼ in. March, 1914, 5 ft. 7 in. and 139 lbs. November, 1914, 5 ft. 7¼ in.

Candidate rejected in December for short height and defective vision, but in March for short height and *light weight.*

Geo. F. Doherty (3415)

January, 1914, 5 ft. 7½ in., 139 lbs., rejected. March, 1914, 5 ft. 7½ in., 140 lbs., passed. November, 1914, 5 ft. 7 3/5 in., 139½ lbs.

Wm. V. Ford (3416)

January, 1914, 5 ft. 10½ in., 147 lbs. March, 1914, 5 ft. 10½ in., 156 lbs. November, 1914, 5 ft. 10½ in., 144 lbs., *dressed.*

In December, 1913, the candidate was rejected for light weight which was made up in March, but he lost more than ever by the next November.

Wm. J. Hawthorn (3419)

December, 1913, 5 ft. 7¼ in., rejected. March, 1914, 5 ft. 7 in. November, 1914, 5 ft. 7 in.

S. C. McFarland (3420)

March, 1914, 5 ft. 7½ in. November, 1914, 5 ft. 7 3/5 in.

C. H. Goldberg (3421)

December, 1913, 5 ft. 10½ in. November, 1914, 5 ft. 11 plus.

Philip J. Rudishauber (3426)

Rejected December, 1913, for flat foot; on examination by Dr. Warbasse for the State Commission November, 1914, *no* flat foot was found. He is member of National Guard and three years ago passed his examination, including feet.

John A. Reinold (3428)

February, 1914, rejected by Dr. Warbasse for flat foot; examined November, 1914, and *no* flat foot found; took no treatment of any kind.

Frank Anglin (3432)

Same kind of case.

Ernest C. Drosher (3434)

Rejected December, 1913, for defective vision; November, 1914, *no* fault found.

Joseph Mayer, Jr. (3434)

Same kind of case. Witness testified that after his rejection in March, 1914, he went to the eye and ear hospital in 64th street and the physicians there could find no fault in his eyes.

Geo. M. Bolles (3437)

Rejected December, 1913, for flat foot and insufficient chest expansion. In November, 1914, Dr. Warbasse finds insufficient chest expansion but *no* fault with feet.

Jas. F. McKenna (3439)

January, 1914, rejected for flat foot. November, 1914, declared to have defective eyesight; but no fault found with feet of candidate; had passed examination at Navy Yard — *no* flat foot.

E. H. Lehman (3442)

January, 1914, rejected, defective chest expansion, but passed March, 1914, and *no* fault found November, 1914.

These men were examined November, 1914, and the same findings as before, to wit: (3447); A. G. Gustaveson, Robt. J. Kelly, Chas. J. Huberer, Jos. E. Kiegan.

TABLE "C"

Cases in Finger Print Examination

Witnesses

Gottlieb (542, 838, 849); Kuhne (617, 643, 807); Sullender (636, 643, 656, 758, 815); Merchant (682–5); Horn (812); Mairs (822); Scott (841, 851, 864); McNulty (858, 871); Protest (884); O'Farrell (889); Hughes (897); Zlinkoff (1095); Mirel (1119); Liddell (1122); Kelly (1126); Morell (1132); Dr. De Forrest (644, 703, 886, 856, 870); Mr. Taylor (6821); Examiner Ireland (938).

Letters

Containing details of complaints concerning the examination (5201), by Rutherford Lewis, Metta F. Merchant, Chas. W. King, I. Aronowitz, H. F. Lawlor, Geo. T. Chattaway, John A. Harrahill, A. A. Saeger, Chas. Juengst, C. E. Donnelly, Henry Weinberger, Wm. D. Collins, C. F. Ehrentreich, Otto A. Scholz, B. J. Lally, J. Lyendecker, Geo. Conroy, Richard Zaworski, Thos. R. Healy, Frank Firner, R. J. Corcoran, Wm. A. Purnhagen, John J. Sullivan, Edward F. McCormack, Wm. H. Fielding, Paul Kizenberger, Blanche A. Donohue, Florence G. Hayes, Edward Christ, S. P. Murphy, John A. Byron, Edward J. Daly, Geo. Elze, James G. Glennon, Thomas Fitzpatrick, Jr., Wm. E. Barrett.

TABLE "D"

Cases in Connection with the Forty-seven Special Charity Examiners

1. Cases of harsh dealing with poor people by some of the forty-seven alleged social service charity examiners.
2. Special forty-seven examiners and their qualifications.
3. Individuals on old eligible list who were passed over when the forty-seven were appointed.
4. Comparative figures, etc., and other matters.

TABLE "D" (1)

Cases of Harsh Dealing with Poor People By Some of the Forty-seven Examiners of Charitable Institutions Appointed Without Competitive Examination

Page 1103. Mezeita Bellantoni, idiot boy forced back from Children's Hospital into a poor Italian family, and compelled to live with a large family of children in squalid and heart-breaking circumstances.

Page 1111. Mary Grassa, daughter, 40 years old, mentally defective; mother directed to pay $4 per month for her maintenance on Randall's Island; without sufficient means of support and scarcely any income.

Page 1139. Lettie Luisi, "little mother" of family of seven children; compelled to pay $4 per month for care of brother on Randall's Island, they wanted $7 "week," she said. (Probably meant month.)

Page 1147. Isidor Friedman, paralyzed child on Randall's Island; one of two children at home paralyzed; told to pay $1 weekly for care of child or father would be "sent to Blackwell's Island."

Page 1155. Joseph Brown, five-year old child on Randall's Island; ordered to pay $8 per month or father would be "taken to the law."

Page 1163. Lizzie Kerner, has boy 15 years old on Randall's Island; told to pay $16 per month; compelled to pay $12; paid $6 on instalment; couldn't pay more; she lives on fourth floor of tenement and works to maintain family.

Page 1179. David Schorr, child on Randall's Island; wife dead; sleeps in his one room shop; ordered to pay $2 weekly; told he would " get arrested " if he stopped payment; paid $5 for one month; can't earn enough to live on.

Page 1189. O. J. Schutzman, ordered to pay $2 weekly on threat of being taken to court; paid $4 per month for two months; can't pay anything.

Page 1195. Samuel Papier, has six children at home; two epileptic; ordered to pay $3 weekly for child on Randall's Island; summoned to court and must report to probation officer weekly.

Page 1298. Mrs. A. Meyerhoff, 66 years old; takes in washing to earn living; widow, 25 years; compelled to pay $5 monthly for daughter on Randall's Island.

Page 1299. Annie O'Brien, ordered to pay $8 monthly for daughter on Randall's Island; told if she didn't pay, she would have to take child home; also threatened with the law.

Page 1483. Hilma Mustonem, janitress in tenement house; boy on Randall's Island; cripple and paralyzed; ordered to pay $2 weekly or would send child back to Finland; paid $5 for one month; can't pay more.

Page 1483. Helen Bonzan, domestic; boards with friends; ordered to pay $5 monthly or take child away; said she " took the money from her mouth " (meaning food); deserted by husband; no home.

Page 1577. Christian Roesch — told to pay at least $10 monthly for sister on Randall's Island or sister would be sent away; couldn't afford more than $5; compelled to pay $10.

Page 1766. Special Reinvestigation Bureau tried to compel the discharge of Elizabeth and Edward Corrigan from St. Malachy's Home to relatives. Case reconsidered on protest of Father Higgins of Catholic Home Bureau and action rescinded.

Page 1809. Special Reinvestigation Bureau ordered the dismissal of Donald and Harold Clark from the Orphan Home, Brooklyn. Action was rescinded on protest of Father Higgins.

Page 1821. Alexander and George Costigan ordered discharged from the Convent of the Sisters of Mercy to a place outside the State; and certificate of removal given without consulting State Board of Charities; action rescinded after protest of Father Higgins.

Page 1841. Special Reinvestigation Bureau ordered discharge of boy known on the record as "Thomas V." to mother whose character was questionable. Action rescinded after protest of Father Higgins.

Page 1853. Special Reinvestigation Bureau ordered discharge of "John and Joseph C." from Convent of Mercy, to parent of questionable character. Action rescinded after protest of Father Higgins.

Page 1863. Special Reinvestigation Bureau ordered discharge of Hattie, Bertha and Gertrude Drehs from Orphan Home to mother who was living with a man who she said was second husband, but failed to produce marriage certificate. Children remained in institution because of protest of Father Higgins.

Page 1878. William French, 11 years old was ordered discharged from St. John's Home by Special Reinvestigation Bureau. *Boy set fire four times to his mother's and sister's home after discharge and was committed to Randall's Island as mental defective.*

Page 2135. Maria Trezza, 16 year old boy, helpless paralytic discharged from Randall's Island because he could not pay "$10 weekly." Charities Department says this should be $10 monthly. Was asked to pay $5 monthly; could not do it, and took boy home.

Page 2223. Sam Engelstein, son 12 years old, sent from Randall's Island into family of six children; boy violent and mental defective. Ordered to pay to keep the child on Randall's Island; said he was impoverished and could not pay. Was told to take child home.

Page 2357. Nathan Wandruff, ordered to take 7 year old son from Randall's Island or pay $5 monthly. Signed agreement to pay $5 though he could not read English; can't pay the money.

Page 2525. Kate Manneback, widow, whose sister, Mrs. Emscher, also widow, has three children in St. Michael's Home, Staten Island; Mrs. Emscher is in Consumptive's Home. Special Reinvestigation Bureau wanted children taken from home and investigator suggested they would be "sent out West" if they were not removed.

Page 6296. Mrs. Dora London, Special Reinvestigation Bureau wanted Mrs. Dora London to take her two children out of charitable institution and suggested they would be deported if she did not do so. Threat was withdrawn after remonstrance by United Hebrew Charities.

These were sample cases; many others were reported to the Commissioners.

In connection with these cases see testimony of Ida M. Robins, 1694, 1783, 2444; Mary Dunphy, 1495, 1538; Max Niklas, 1504, 1547, 1656; A. P. Thorne, 1588, 1668, 2353, 2438; F. R. Bauer, 1670; Katherine A. Ward, 1896; Dr. Schlapp, 2185, 2211.

TABLE "D" (2)

EXAMINATION OF SOME OF THE NEW FORTY-SEVEN EXAMINERS AND THEIR QUALIFICATIONS

Page 2258. Bernardine Sherman.
Page 2292. Mrs. G. Gleason.
Page 2320–34. Edith Holman.
Page 2366. Matthew Spalletta.
Page 2388. Florence Baldwin.
Page 2410. Miss B. Irvine.
Page 2442–43. Charline E. Mayfield.
Page 2447. Laura C. Tobey.
Page 2470. Nellie Wise.
Page 2491. Mary Tinney.
Page 2509. Clara B. Flynn.
Page 2530. Eva A. Marty.
Page 2555. Max Rothschild.
Page 2569. Mary J. Van Hook.

TABLE "D" (3)

EXAMINATION OF INDIVIDUALS ON THE OLD ELIGIBLE LIST WHO WERE PASSSED OVER WITH OTHERS

Page 2620. Elizabeth Mulholland.
2733. Catharine Haenlein.
2736. Mary F. Rita.
2748. Elizabeth A. Butler.
2760. Elizabeth Stevens.
3137. Julia Ryan.

Page 3260. Mary O'Connor.
3294. Cora Woelters.
3384. Mary F. Martin.
6179. Louise E. Webber.

TABLE "D" (4)

Comparative statements and figures showing that "Social Service" could *not* be undertaken on basis of appropriation asked for by Charities Commissioner.

EXTRACTS FROM STATEMENT SUBMITTED TO FINANCE DEPARTMENT, PREPARED BY H. B. DINWIDDIE, GENERAL INSPECTOR, CHARITIES DEPARTMENT, ON WHICH REQUEST FOR FUNDS FOR FORTY-SEVEN SPECIAL INSPECTORS WAS BASED

An analysis of the work of the Bureau of Dependent Adults, Brooklyn, for the first two months of the year 1914 shows that the average number of cases completed in a full day for each examiner in the field was only a *trifle over 6.* Although the field work in Brooklyn would naturally require an Examiner to cover more territory than in the congested districts of Manhattan, it is felt that this average number of cases could be *increased.*

* * * * * * * * *

As the basis of the need for additional employees lies in the additional amount of field work to be undertaken, an effort was made to compute the number of field examiners first. The estimate of the number of other employees needed was then based upon the number of additional field examiners required. The complete showing for all employees needed will be found in Table X. The number of employees of each class needed will be found there also, both collectively and separately by bureaus.

* * * * * * * * *

The class of dependents excepted above as calling for more than one investigation is the children in the Children's Hospitals on Randall's Island. In view of the experience in the reinvestigation in the children's work in the Children's Bureaus for the different boroughs, it has seemed economical and important that a *quarterly investigation* should be made of the family conditions of these children. The number of children whose relatives or friends cannot be located upon annual investigation by the Children's Bureaus is large. In the years 1911, 1912 and 1913 the Children's Bureaus in Manhattan and in Brooklyn were "unable to locate at address given" the relatives or friends of committed children in from 18 to 31 per cent. of the cases annually. A total of 8,470 cases of children for *reinvestigation* was involved.

* * * * * * * * *

It has been the rule of the Department of Public Charities to make an investigation of these *children annually.*

* * * * * * * * *

In Tables I and X, appended to this report it will be found that the number of persons involved in the initial reinvestigation in the Department institutions for the Bureau of Dependent Adults, Manhattan, was 8,390. At the rate of *11.45 cases for a day* of full work for an examiner, this would necessitate 724 full days of work in investigation. Assuming that the additional staff will be allowed for six months' work in 1914, there would be 5.5 examiners needed for this particular work in the 132 full days' work in the half year.

* * * * * * * * *

The number of dependents to be *reinvestigated* in the Municipal hospitals in Kings county will be found from Tables V and X to have been 2,441. These 2,441 cases would require the time of an additional examiner and .8 of the time of another one for six months.

* * * * * * * * *

In the private hospitals there were also 795 patients remaining January 31, 1914 that had been accepted as public charges by the Brooklyn Bureau of Dependent Adults. To investigate these at the rate *of 10 cases a day* would require .6 of an examiner's time for six months. (See Tables VI and X.)

* * * * * * * * *

There were 1,236 such public charges remaining in institutions that had been accepted by the Manhattan Bureau of Dependent Adults on January 31, 1914 (see Tables III and X). At the rate of 11.45 cases a day, it would take .8 of an examiner's time for six months to do this work. The supplementary quarterly reinvestigation would include only the inmates of the institutions for special treatment of children who had been public charges for three months and over. There were 280 such children as will be seen from Table III. At the rate of *10 completed cases per day,* it would require .2 of an examiner's time to make a quarterly reinvestigation of those cases within six months.

There were 578 inmates remaining in the private institutions for the special treatment of children and in the institutions for unmarried mothers and friendless women on January 31, 1914, who had been accepted as public charges by the Bureau in Brooklyn. At the rate *of 10 cases a day,* it would require .4 of an examiner's time in six months to investigate these. (See Tables VII and X).

* * * * * * * * *

There were 171 tuberculosis, cancer, chronic and home cases remaining in private institutions on January 31, 1914, which had been accepted as public charges by the Brooklyn Bureau. At the rate of *10 cases per day,* it would take .1 of an examiner's time to complete this work in six months. (See Tables VIII and X).

* * * * * * * * *

There were remaining in child-caring institutions on January 31, 1914, 12,418 children that had been committed by the Children's Bureau, Manhattan. The ratio of children to the families involved is about 2 to 1, according to the recent annual reports of the Bureau. This would make about 6,209 families to be reinvestigated. At the rate *of 6 investigations a day,* it would take 7.8 examiners to do this work in six months. (See Table X.)

According to the proportions found among the children committed by the Brooklyn Bureau of Dependent Children remaining in institutions on January 31, 1914, three months and over, 11,308 of the 12,418 committed by the Manhattan Bureau had been in the institutions over three months, representing an estimated number of 5,654 families. To make a supplementary quarterly investigation of these at the *rate of 6 cases a day* would require the time of 7.1 examiners for six months. (See Tables IX and X.)

* * * * * * * * *

TESTIMONY OF COMPTROLLER WILLIAM A. PRENDERGAST (PAGE 4351)

Q. It would appear from this report, Mr. Prendergast, that the transfer of $50,000 from the food supplies appropriation to this particular need was an unusual transfer, and was recommended upon special grounds. Have you a recollection of that? A. I have a very clear recollection of the entire transaction, sir, as I am largely responsible, in fact I might say wholly responsible for it, and it was done under my direction.

Q. The purpose of making that transfer in order that these appointments might be made, as you understood it, was that of *economy,* was it not, and the saving of money to the city through the removal of dependents from institutions who did not belong there? A. The purpose of the transfer are fully explained in the reports and deal with *that very point,* Mr. Moss.

Q. Was there anything else, Mr. Comptroller, that was present in your mind in making these recommendations besides that which was suggested in the report? A. *Certainly not.*

Q. No other purposes were expressed to you in the conferences that you had with fellow members of the city administration, or the board of estimate, no other purpose than that which is expressed in the report? A. *None whatever.*

TESTIMONY OF WOLF SCHEINBERG, EXAMINER IN FINANCE DEPARTMENT (PAGE 4386)

Q. Did you investigate the request of the Charities Commissioner Kingsbury, for the transfer of funds for the purpose of appointing additional examiners of charitable institutions made by him on June 26th last? A. Yes.

Q. What investigation did you make? A. I read the report of the General Inspector Dunwoodie, and then went over to the Bureau of Dependent Adults and Children, and made a partial study of the number of applicants for the city's charity, especially those with respect to the children and the public charges for the purpose of getting a fair estimate of how many people would be required to make the *reinvestigation* that was contemplated by the Department, the way I understood it in their request (p. 4388).

Q. You found that there were needs for that additional *reinvestigator force?* A. *For this work?*

Q. For this particular work. A. For this particular work.

Testimony of Edward T. Devine, Director of Social Investigation in the Department of Charities (Page 6382)

Q. Do you know Miss Ida M. Cannon? A. Yes.

Q. Did she estimate ten cases a month of complete social service? A. I do not know. I have not seen that report.

* * * * * * * * * * * * * * *

Q. Do you remember a representative of the Finance Departmen who called at the office of the Charity Organization? A. I do not remember that, no.

Q. If he reported that the C. O. S. thought that thirty cases could be completed a month, would he be right, or about right? A. I think the answer I have already given would apply to that. If you mean the kinds of investigation which the Charity Organization Society make with reference to the kind of help that they try to give, then I think it would be perfectly possible to answer that; *I should say that thirty is rather a high estimate.*

Q. You think it is less than that? A. Yes, but I think ten is too low an estimate, but it certainly depends on the kind of a decision that you have to make; what it is you are trying to do? One investigation might require two or three days, and another might require only a couple of hours.

Testimony of Henry Moskowitz, President Municipal Civil Service Commission (Page 4439)

Q. Did you see a copy of the report that Comptroller Prendergast submitted to the Board of Estimate when it passed the final resolution? A. I do not think I did then, no.

Q. Did you know that the request to the Board of Estimate was simply for reinvestigators; that the request made of the Board of estimate was simply for reinvestigators? A. Reinvestigation.

* * * * * * * * * * * * * * *

Q. The question is, Mr. President, did you know it? A. Did I know it? I did not know it then, but if I had known it, Mr. Moss, *it would not have made any difference.*

Reinvestigation plus social service at the rate of 30 *cases a month would have required the services of* 700 *investigators.*

Mrs. Ida P. Upshaw, Superintendent of the Bureau of Domestic Relations, of the Charities Department, furnished the State Commission with her report for the year 1914, which shows that 5,198 cases of abandonment and nonsupport were settled out of court during that year. The work of family rehabilitation had been carried on by Mrs. Upshaw in this bureau for many years.

The report of the Desertion Bureau of the United Hebrew Charities shows that 1,875 family deserters were traced in various parts of the country during the past three years; that 575 of them were reunited to their families and support was obtained from 427 of them for the families they deserted (pp. 6527–9).

Family rehabilitation is carried on by virtually every private charitable organization in the city.

APPENDIX

Wood-block Paving Monopoly

The testimony of Mr. Wild, with his references to engineers Sullivan and Durham, the references to Mr. Dow, the fact that consulting engineer Goodrich is the controlling engineering head of the department in Manhattan and takes full responsibility for the specifications for wood-block paving, and the fact that in the directions that have opened to us it is clear that the department in Manhattan is running in contempt of the Civil Service Law when it affects friends and cliques, and that until lately the Borough President did not know of these violations — he now has begun to secure control of these positions, which will eliminate illegal and disadvantageous conditions — these facts show that a discussion of wood-block paving in its relation to officials who stretch and violate the Civil Service Law, is entirely in order.

Wood-block paving has been laid in New York City in large quantities, and its use is on the increase. It is less noisy than granite, and more enduring than asphalt. The subject is of great importance and *we felt it to be our duty to follow the line that opened,* related so closely as it is to the vital subject of the administration of the Civil Service Law. On this topic we examined witnesses of prime importance. Consulting engineer, Goodrich (p. 5258), and Mr. Wild were carefully examined; the eminent engineers, James W. Howard (p. 5409), and Richard E. Lamb (p. 5511), and a prominent manufacturer, A. E. Mitchell (p. 5464), and towards the end of the inquiry Mr. Goodrich returned and brought a manufacturer of oil, Mr. P. C. Reilly. They were examined and Mr. Howard and Mr. Lamb were recalled.

The element considered was the oil with which the wood blocks are saturated under heat and pressure to preserve them. Mr. Howard and Mr. Lamb showed that the notable wooden pavements which have endured for many years, such as Michigan Boulevard, Chicago, and Tremont street, Boston, were treated with oils from which the pitch was largely eliminated and which were high in creosote and other chemical qualities. They said that there is a combination of companies *with interlocking directorates,* the members of which were shown, and that a combination of these companies sued by the United States Government was ordered to dissolve; that they produce an oil, which is derived from the coal-tar by-product of coke ovens throughout the country operated under certain patents, the royalty for which is this particular by-product; also from gas works which largely are operated in harmony with the others.

This by-product contains a large proportion of pitch which is useless and even deleterious for paving uses, but which if extracted would be unsalable in this part of the country, and of little value anywhere, though of large bulk. The problem for the producers of this product is to save the expense of removing the pitch, and to get a price for it. This is accomplished by including it in the oil. Such an oil was not used in the streets above mentioned, nor in the excellent old pavement on Broadway between Bowling Green and Trinity church. There are no illustrations of good pavements, maintained for many years, where this "pitch oil" was used. When such an oil is to be marketed for wood-paving in the cities, it must be *included* in the specifications, and if possible the other (clean) oil must be *excluded.*

Ingenious chemists have devised formulas for specifications designed to look like careful protection, but really to specify pitch oil. Those engineers who have been employed to help the so-called " Trust " may be found going to the various cities on such missions. They argue for a heavy oil (always meaning a pitch oil such as the " trust " manufactures and sells), but they have difficulty in producing expert testimony for it except out of their own set. The connections of men in various cities who work for the pitch oils are interesting.

Out of the warfare have come two terms well recognized among engineers, " closed specifications," and " open specifications." Those terms were admitted by Mr. Goodrich. " Closed specifications " are those which favor the heavy (pitch) oils by various static and chemical tests; " open specifications " give the alternative privilege of bidding for two kinds of oil, one heavy (pitchy); the other light. The trust has so great an influence that it has prevented any specifications that are closed to heavy oils; the alternative specification is the only chance for the lighter oil, and that oil which is more highly refined has to compete with the pitch oil, even under open specifications. It was maintained by Mr. Mitchell, president of the Wyckoff Pipe and Creosoting Company, that under the closed specifications it is substantially impossible for manufacturers and contractors to supply wooden paving blocks, *except as treated by the heavy oil* which, he maintained, was substantially controlled by the trust. Mr. Howard and Mr. Lamb supported him in that claim.

Mr. Mitchell showed by facts, figures and personal experiences, the truth of his claim, and he exhibited a long correspondence of protest with the *former borough president, who relied entirely upon Mr. Goodrich,* and followed the course laid down by Mr. Goodrich in the use of the specification which Mr. Howard and Mr. Lamb as engineers said, with Mr. Mitchell the manufacturer, substantially closed out all but pitch oil, *the oil of the trust.* It was shown that in New York City only Richmond borough has open specifications, and Mr. Mitchell and Mr. Lamb said they were able to compete and to work there. Some work done by Mr. Lamb in Brooklyn was done with a small quantity of oil that he had secured for a job at Atlantic City under closed specifications, which oil in a limited amount he obtained from a trust subsidiary by a little shrewdness.

It was shown by Mr. Howard that in the cities which have good and progressive governments, the open specification is used, and that usually the presence of the *closed specification* is found in a city where the government is selfish and *under suspicion.* He said the presence of the closed specifications is sufficient to raise suspicion.

The qualifications of these three witnesses are extraordinary in their knowledge of the subject and their experience in the cities of the United States and in Europe, and *their position has been maintained by authorities and by the decisions of engineering bodies.*

As a part of the statements of these three witnesses amounted to an allegation that through these specifications the coal-tar-trust has a virtual monopoly of the oil that must be used, Mr. Goodrich tried to refute that suggestion. He said (1) he had found that the required oil can be obtained from the Kettle River Company, located in the West, and (2) from Europe. He couldn't give figures or facts, or any report, or any transactions, but said the statement was based on an investigation which he made and reported orally to the former borough president (who undoubtedly believed him).

Mr. Lamb, however, showed from his personal detailed experience that help from Europe (even before the war) was practically and commercially *impossible;* as for the other, during our investigation, a telegram was sent to the Kettle River Company asking if they would sell some of their oil, and they responded that they *would not sell any oil but that they had delivered our telegram to the Barrett Company which would answer us directly. The Barrett Company is the head and front of the Trust!*

Mr. Goodrich produced Mr. Reilly, the head of the Republic Company, which he said was not in the Trust. Mr. Reilly said he had a large independent company and manufactured his own oil from the tar which he bought direct from the coke ovens and gas houses. He said that with this oil which he produced from these materials, he was able to compete successfully in New York city and to get contracts. He admitted that a light oil which he manufactured could not be used. The point of his testimony was an attempted refutation of the suggestion of a trust control. But his *testimony failed to touch the case* because he said he obtained the oil from the same ovens from which the Trust buys; and he mentioned one of the plants located in Indianapolis, which is *operating under the very patents which form the basis of the Trust combination.*

An interesting fact appeared in this — that in the contract for heavy oil for Broad street, Newark, which was made over the mayor's veto, the blocks used were furnished by one contractor, who obtained them equally from Mr. Reilly's Republic Company, and the American Creosoting Company — which is in the Trust combination. It appeared that a number of years ago Mr. Reilly fought the Trust for a chance to do business, and it is evident that the companies now find it to their interest to allow Mr. Reilly to buy the oil he needs, without interference. But Mr. Mitchell and Mr. Lamb have found it impossible to get a supply fit for the needs of business.

The short time at our disposal and the natural limitation of the subject of inquiry, prevented us from developing the connections of persons associated in these matters. Further information on this line was not used for the purposes of the inquiry and of the report.

New York (State)
Civil service
commission

... Report of an
investigation...

www.ingramcontent.com/pod-product-compliance
Lightning Source LLC
LaVergne TN
LVHW021359110826
845150LV00007B/1711

* 9 7 8 1 4 2 5 5 1 3 1 1 5 *